Raleigh Bell was a naval aviator in the 1960s who roomed with aviators who were in the Battle of Midway. What some saw and learned gave him the interest to write this story. The author explains that this was a battle we shouldn't have won and if we had lost, what weapons Germany had that might have changed the outcome of World War II. If the Japanese had won this battle, what pressure would have been on President Roosevelt to protect the West Coast of the United States?

Raleigh Bell

JAPANESE VICTORY AT MIDWAY
WHAT IF?

AUSTIN MACAULEY PUBLISHERS™

LONDON * CAMBRIDGE * NEW YORK * SHARJAH

Ordering Information
Quantity sales: Special discounts are available on quantity purchases by corporations, associations, and others. For details, contact the publisher at the address below.

Publisher's Cataloging-in-Publication data
Bell, Raleigh
Japanese Victory at Midway What If?

ISBN 9798886936193 (Paperback)
ISBN 9798886936209 (ePub e-book)

Library of Congress Control Number: 2023914892

www.austinmacauley.com/us

First Published 2024
Austin Macauley Publishers LLC
40 Wall Street, 33rd Floor, Suite 3302
New York, NY 10005
USA

mail-usa@austinmacauley.com
+1 (646) 5125767

Table of Contents

Prologue

We Could Be Speaking German?

"Midway was one of the most decisive naval battles of all time. It was a battle that should have been won by the Japanese but wasn't." Historian Thomas Wildenberg.[1]

The American assault on the Japanese fleet at Midway was "the single most decisive aerial attack in naval history," according to historians Jonathan B. Parshall and Anthony P. Tully.[2]

"They had no right to win, yet they did, and in so doing changed the course of the war." Walter Lord in his Incredible Victory.[3]

Many historians place the Battle of Midway as one of the most important battles in world history. This author finds it to be the most important in all of American history and as you read these pages you will find that if this battle had been lost, what would have happened to this great country, called America?

What would have changed if the Japanese did win the Battle of Midway?

The Chief of Naval Operations, Admiral Harold Stark submitted his Plan Dog memo for confronting a two-front war against Germany and Italy in Europe and Japan in the Pacific. This memo discussed the use of Rainbow 5 for a two-front war taking defensive action against the Japanese until Germany and Italy could be defeated.

Admiral Stark presented his Plan Dog memo to President Roosevelt, who then adopted the Europe First approach to World War II, which was also favored by the British. It was thought that Germany was a greater threat and the war in the Pacific with the Japanese could be held off until Germany was defeated.

"That those threats to the American way of life and the interests of the United States in Europe, Latin America, and the Far East against which threats the huge new defense program of this country is directed all stem, in the last analysis from the power of Nazi Germany."[4]

Within the United States, German action was causing concerns among businessmen, bankers, farmers, educators, and government officials that the war in Europe was a threat to the economy of the United States. They didn't see the threat from Japan the same way. They felt that Germany's occupation of Western Europe significantly reduced the volume of trade flowing between European and American ports. Plus exports of agricultural products were harming American farmers. They viewed Nazi Germany's economic move into Central American as a threat to the Western Hemisphere which was not in the best interest of American values and interests.

"The Atlantic world, unless it destroys itself, will remain infinitely superior in vigor and inventive power to the too prolific and not too well-nourished Orientals."[5]

"Since Germany is the predominant member of the Axis Powers, the Atlantic and European area is considered to be the decisive theatre. The principal United States Military effort will be exerted in that theatre." [6]

The Europe First adoption for World War II was affirmed by President Roosevelt at the Arcadia Conference in Washington in December 1941. Britain's Prime Minister Winston Churchill had arrived in Washington after the Japanese had attacked Oahu to make sure that American was still focused on Europe first.

Japanese Plans for Midway

Knowing that the surprise attack on the Hawaii island of Oahu on 7 December 1941 did not destroy any American carriers, the Japanese leaders knew to control the Pacific, they had to sink those carriers and a plan to do so included Midway.

The Japanese plans for capturing Midway and the destruction of the rest of the U.S. Navy fleet in the Pacific was to push the United States out of the Pacific long enough for the Japanese Empire to established superiority in the Pacific. To accomplish this after Midway they had to capture Hawaii or use their air power from their carriers to control what forces came into and out of Pearl Harbor. This would open the American west coast to possible attacks.

If this occurred, President Roosevelt would be forced to move naval units from the Atlantic to the Pacific coast and relocate army units bounded for

Europe to protect the west coast from possible Japanese attacks. This decision could have affected his Europe First policy and therefore the outcome of the war.

If the Japanese had won the battle of Midway and controlled the Pacific, President Roosevelt's re-location of naval forces from the Atlantic to the Pacific would have taken more time and could have affected the Atlantic convoy patrols. Although the United States Navy had more destroyers in the Atlantic and 30 at Pearl Harbor on 7 December, only three were damaged but repaired. They probably could have continued the Atlantic patrols without sending any destroyers to the Pacific except to escort other ships being moved to the Pacific area from the west coast or through the Panama Canal.

The Canadian navy was aiding with the Atlantic convoys and after the Japanese attack at Pearl Harbor, they had been forced to give the Pacific theatre a higher priority. The only Canadian force of any size that they had on the west coast was the Fishermen's Reserve, which wasn't a part of the real Canadian navy. Many called the Fishermen's Reserve a navy within a navy. After the Japanese attack on Pearl Harbor the number of vessels for the Fishermen's Reserve was 48; comprise mostly of local fishing vessels, and 475 men drawn from the local fishing communities. This group operated out of Prince Rupert, Vancouver, and Esquimalt on tip of Vancouver Island, close to Victoria.[7]

If Roosevelt was forced to move forces, it could have changed his Europe First policy with Great Britain and the planned invasion of France at Normandy with Operation Overlord in June 1944.

Although the Allies landing on Normandy was a success, allowing the Allies forces to move from battle to battle to victory in Berlin on 7 May 1945, a delay in this landing may have allowed Germany to bring one or more of their secret weapons against the Allies, possibly changing the course of the war.

At this time in history, Germany may have had the best scientists in the world. Many of these scientists had completed or were still working on a long list of secret weapons, including the atomic bomb and an aircraft that might have reached the east coast of the United States. The most promising of their weapons was the V-2 rocket. This weapon had proven successful against England and now their scientists were taking that technology and creating a two-stage A10 rocket that was called the Amerika Rocket, meant for the mainland of the United States. This A10 had been tested in March 1945 and if the war had continued, could have been a serious weapon against the U.S. They were also working on long-range bombers which could possible reach the U.S. east coast. If the war was extended, Germany may have introduced these weapons and changed the course of the war. The Germans also had some strange weapons in their design stage and are discussed in a later chapter.

"It was rightly feared that if the war in the West was unduly prolonged, German scientists would invent secret weapons that would prove irresistible… There was no time to lose in eliminating German science from the war. There was no comparable peril from Japanese science."[8]

A look at what was going on in Japan, China, Germany, Britain, and the United States at this time, plus the German secret weapons in development that could affect the war, gives an excellent overview of how the war could have changed if the Japanese had a victory at the Battle of Midway.

We could be speaking German.

Chapter 1
Fear of Invasion

At the Japanese Imperial Conference on 6 September 1941, just three months before Pearl Harbor, the Japanese military leadership presented a document called "The Essentials for Carrying Out the Empire's Policies." This document produced a series of questions and answers. One question was: "What is the outlook in a war with Great Britain and the United States, particularly, how shall we end the war?"

The document produced from this conference states the demands Japan will make of the United States, Great Britain and the Netherlands through their diplomatic efforts first and if those failed, Japan would proceed with war with these three countries.

The answer given was a war with the United States and Great Britain will be long and will become a war of endurance. It is very difficult to predict the termination of any war and it would be well-nigh impossible to expect the surrender of the United States. However, we cannot exclude the possibility that the war could end because of a great change in American public opinion, which may result from such factors as the remarkable success of our military operations in the South or the surrender of Great Britain of their parts of the British Empire in Southeast Asia. At any rate, we should be able to establish an invincible position by building up a strategically advantageous position through the occupation of important areas in the South, by creating an economy that will be self-sufficient in the long run through the development of rich resources in the Southern regions, as well as through the use of the economic power of the East Asian continent; and by linking Asia and Europe in destroying the Anglo-American coalition through our cooperation with Germany and Italy. Meanwhile, we may hope that we will be able to influence the trend of affairs and bring the war to an end.[1]

Speaking at the same conference, Admiral Osami Nagano; the Chief of Staff of the Imperial Japanese Navy said, "Since Japan is unavoidable facing a national ruin whether it decides to fight the United States or submit to its demands, it must by all means chose to fight." He continued, "Japan would rather go down fighting than ignobly surrender without a struggle because surrender would spell spiritual as well as a physical ruin for the nation and its destiny."[2]

Meeting again on 1 December, the Japanese Imperial Conference decided to go to war with the United States, Great Britain, and the Netherlands as all had holdings in areas of the Pacific that Japan want to occupy. Upon this decision, the Japanese Emperor Hirohito issued orders to Admiral Isoroku Yamamoto, commander in chief of the Japanese Combine, Fleet. This fleet was the main sea-going component of the Japanese Navy and would be responsible for conducting all Japanese Navy orders received from the emperor.

The emperor's statement read, "You must be determined to meet our expectations by exalting our force and authority throughout the world by annihilating the enemy." Much discussion after the war questioned whether the emperor was involved in the war but this statement made it clear that the emperor was involved in the conduct of the war effort.

The Japanese military had their orders, war it was.

In early 1941, Admiral Yamamoto wrote a letter to the Minister of the Japanese Navy, Koshiro Oikawa strongly urging the implementation of his Hawaii operation in which he said, "In a war between Japan and the U.S., the first essential matter to be carried out is to furiously attack and destroy the enemy fleet at the beginning of the war. This can cause the U.S. Navy and the American people to lose their morale to such an extent they will never get it back…We must strive extremely hard to make the best of a war between Japan and the U.S.…We thus need to be determined to win or lose the war on the first day…"[3]

After its successful attack on 7 December 1941, Admiral Yamamoto knew that the American carriers were not at Pearl and had to be destroyed for the Japanese to be successful in the Pacific. His operations officers, led by his chief of staff Rear Admiral Matome Ugaki developed a plan called Eastern Operation.

Under this plan it called for the capture of Midway, drawing out and destroying the American carriers; which has escaped the attack on 7 December at Pearl Harbor, the capture of Johnston Atoll; located about 860 miles southwest of the Hawaii Islands. They planned to use the Johnston Atoll as a staging area for the invasion of Hawaii. The plan was to capture the Big Island Hawaii, establish airbases on it and other of the outer islands from which they could launch attacks against Oahu. The Japanese army disapproved of this plan as it would have stretched out the army from its supply sources.[4]

The Japanese became concerned after the Doolittle raid in March 1942 and wanted to increase their defensive sphere. They agreed to a deal from Admiral Yamamoto, the Japanese army would provide troops for the invasion of Midway, and that several divisions of the Japanese army had been ordered to prepare for an invasion of the Hawaii Islands.

After the attack on 7 December 1941, Admiral Yamamoto's first proposal was for an invasion of the main Hawaiian Islands. But by earlier February 1942 this plan was modified for invading and occupying Midway Island and certain islands in the Aleutians. Since the attack on Pearl Harbor, the Japanese became aware of the buildup of American forces on Oahu, and the long supply lines required to support an invasion of Oahu was not possible.

The plan for Midway was a plan if they could force a fleet encounter between the Japanese and the United States Navy. Their expected victory at Midway would give the Japanese Empire undisputed control of the central and western Pacific. With no American naval force in the Pacific if the Japanese was successful at Midway, it would have been difficult to stop Japanese control.[5]

After the Japanese surprise attack on Pearl Harbor on 7 December 1941, many civilians and military personnel in Hawaii feared the Japanese might invade Oahu. This included both Admiral Husband Kimmel, Commanding Officer of the Pacific Fleet, and Lt. General Walter Short, commander of U.S. Army Hawaiian Department.

On the morning of 8 December, General George Marshall and his staff met in Washington to determine how to get the Hawaiian garrison back on its feet quickly. They agreed that the Army Air Force had to move enough aircraft to build up the Army air strength to one full group of heavy bombardment and two full groups of pursuit aircraft. By 21 December enough B-17 bombers had flown out of California, bring the heavy bomber strength to a full group at 43 aircraft.[6]

Lieutenant General Walter Short, United States Army, on 8 December 1941 issued a lengthy list of the troops and equipment most urgently needed for the defense of Oahu and by several supplementary lists sent by him during the next few days.

The War Department in Washington began to respond to his request by shipping over 7,000 men, large numbers of ammunition including bombs for aircraft of various sizes from San Francisco. Other convoys followed to bring about 15,000 more troops to Oahu. With these increases, the Hawaiian Department; a division of the U.S. Army, had a strength of about 58,500 officers and enlisted men by the second week in January 1942. They only lacked a serious shortage of antiaircraft weapons. It appeared that Hawaii was now well secured against an invasion.[7]

President Roosevelt and the Joint Chiefs of the military approved the request from the Hawaiian Department for the defense of Hawaii, for 74,000 ground troops to Oahu, 13,000 to the Island of Hawaii, and 12,800 to be distributed among the other five islands. From the beginning of April till the end of June 1942, 106,000 ground and 16,000 air troops were now on the islands of Hawaii. Some of these were used to replace all soldiers of Japanese descent.

Further instructions were for the Navy to maintain 67 patrol aircraft for long-range and local reconnaissance while the Army was to keep 96 heavy, 24 medium and light bombers and 225 fighters.[8]

Food supply became a concern for the islands. When the war started, a normal supply of food was on hand for its 250,000 civilians included an inventory of 37 days of most staples but didn't count the shortages of potatoes, rice, and onions. General Short estimated that they needed a continuing flow of about 32,000 tons of food a month. He asked the War Department to arrange a six-month emergency reserve of 48,000 tons of food.

The islands of Hawaii had little they could provide to the food supply. Its history showed that when the islands were settled by the Polynesians over 1500 years ago that the islands had little that was native. Even pineapples often thought native to the Hawaii Islands were brought by the Spanish in the 18th century. Over the years other fruits, crops, and plants were imported and grown but in 1941 the local food supply barely had enough to feed the local population.

General Short also wanted seeds, fertilizer, insecticides, and farm equipment to be able to increase the growing of crops on the islands.

Fear of Japanese attacks on shipments from the US mainland to Hawaii was a problem which the US Navy had to solve. The Department of the Navy moved the USS Long Island light carrier with naval Task Force One under Admiral Pye along with his seven battleships and some destroyer to protect all naval forces between the west coast and Hawaii. This would allow food to begin to move from San Francisco to Hawaii in late December 1941 and by mid-February 1942 the War Department turned shipments over to the Department of Agriculture.[9]

As the request came for reinforcements for Hawaii, the Navy and War Departments didn't know exactly where the Japanese carriers were and there were thoughts that the Japanese might have a strong navy force including carriers between the west coast and Hawaii. The Navy didn't want any ship movements till this situation was clarified. The Navy assumed that the Japanese had other aircraft carriers free to attack the west coast of the United States. The Army likewise expressed concerns of Japanese attacks on the west coast bomber factories. By 12 December 1941, the Army's position was to take all steps necessary to reinforce the defenses of Oahu without jeopardizing the security of the Continental United States, basically the west coast.[10]

The Navy had a strong opinion that with the added reinforcement of Oahu in December that the Japanese would more likely skip invading Oahu but with their naval air strength, attempt to invade one or more of the undefended outer islands of Hawaii. Once in control of one or more of the outer islands, the Japanese could make attacks against shipping into Oahu and perhaps starve out the population of Oahu. The Navy knowing that their Pacific fleet had suffered greatly on 7 December and couldn't protect all of the outer islands.

The Navy contended that the defense of the Hawaiian area depended primarily on Army airpower and that the security and effectiveness of that airpower required its dispersion among the major islands of the Hawaiian group.[11]

The Japanese had nine submarines operating in the Hawaii area until the middle of January 1942. They wanted to get a better picture of the damage done on 7 December. At dawn on 18 December, they launched an aircraft from one of their submarines and flew over Pearl Harbor. The next day a Japanese message was intercepted; thanks to our cryptanalyst at Station Hypo on Oahu, stating eight battleships, four cruisers and two destroyers had been sunk or heavily damaged with less damage to another battleship and four cruisers. It also claimed 450 aircraft were destroyed on the ground and 14 shot down. Another Japanese flight was carried out on the night of 6-7 January. Neither of these flights was detected by U.S. forces.[12].[13]

The attack by the Japanese continued even after 7 December, just before dust on 15 December a submarine lobbed about ten shells into the harbor of Kahului on Maui. On the night of 30-31 December, Japanese submarines shelled Hilo on the Island of Hawaii, Nawiliwili on the Island of Kauai, and again on Kahului. The damage was limited and no one was injured. But it made all the residents of these islands know that the threat from the Japanese was real and many lived in fear of an invasion by the Japanese at any moment.[14]

General Short was also concerned about the number of Japanese living in Hawaii and their possible support of the Japanese Empire. For defense purposes, he suggested a mass evacuation from Hawaii to another island of Hawaii or the mainland.[15]

On 17 December General Short was replaced by Lt. General Delos C. Emmons. General Emmons assured the War Department in Washington that if a sufficient number of Japanese people living in Hawaii had not been transferred and if an assault was made on Oahu, he had plans to immobilize them.[16]

Knowing that up to 150,000 Japanese from Hawaii might be transferred to the west coast, raised political repercussions from citizens on the west coast and newspapers. Reports in the Honolulu newspapers stated that mass evacuation was impractical. Assistant Secretary of War, Mr. McCloy stated that 1,550 of the most dangerous Japanese would be evacuated.[17]

During December the Navy of necessity recast its Pacific war plans, making the sure control of the Oahu-Midway line, to the north of Oahu, the task was its priority for the Pacific Fleet and giving second priority to that of holding the line from Hawaii to Samoa, south, southwest of Oahu. The necessary corollary of the new strategy outlined for the Pacific Fleet was a much surer defense of Oahu by the United States Army.[18]

On the visit in mid-March 1942, Assistance Secretary of Navy, Mr. McCloy's made a judgment that the Pearl Harbor-Honolulu area still presented a "terribly congested" and "most vulnerable" target.[19]

The Japanese Imperial Navy conceived Operation K. The plan discussed the bombing of California and Texas but the need to get updated information regarding the repairs to US Navy facilities at Pearl after the attack of 7 December was more valuable. By assessing the repairs to the docks, shipyard and airfields would help the Imperial Japanese Navy to determine the ability of the Americans to have the power to fight back over the next several months. Operation K called for the bombing of the docks at Pearl and to disturbing any salvage work.

The operation was to use five Kawanishi H8K "Emily" flying boats with a crew of ten each. The Emily was a long-range aircraft with four-engines designed for patrolling and bombing alone over the ocean.

On the morning of 4 March 942, the Japanese were only able to get two flying boats in the air to start Operation K. The flying boats launched from Jaluit Island in the Marshalls, refueling in a rendezvous with three submarines at French Frigate Shoals and then flown on to Oahu, about 500 miles to the southeast. Army radar picked them up at 90 miles off Kauai, and the Interceptor Command sent up four pursuit planes to find them, but without success because of their high altitude and heavy overcast. One Japanese plane merely skirted the west coast of Oahu. The other followed the north coast to Kaneohe, then turned south and at 2:15 a.m. dropped four 500-pound bombs which landed in woods on the slopes of Mount Tantalus, about 2 miles from downtown Honolulu. They caused no casualties only breaking a few windows. Flying at high altitude and due to the overcast, antiaircraft guns did not fire, and no general air raid alarm was sounded. Both planes returned to their starting point safely; but as a "night reconnaissance" of Pearl Harbor the flight was a failure, and a second "K Operation," as the Japanese called the feat, scheduled for 7 March, was canceled.

This was the longest distance ever undertaken by a two-plane bombing mission, and one of the longest bombing sorties ever planned without fighter escort.

Although American code breakers warned that the Japanese were planning a reconnaissance of Pearl Harbor with refueling at French Frigate Shoals, the superiors ignored the warning.

Later Hawaiian authorities deduced that the Japanese planes must have staged through French Frigate Shoals, and the Navy thereupon took steps to deny them to enemy submarines.[20]

Although there were fears that the Japanese carriers might attack the continental west coast, these fears went away after the U.S. interception of Japanese messages indicated an attack at Midway and the Aleutians.[21]

Another warning about Midway took place six days after the second attack at Pearl Harbor in March when an Emily Flying Boat did a daylight photo-reconnaissance of Midway. The aircraft was incepted by Marine Brewster F2A fighters and destroyed.

General Emmons now having adequate troops and aircraft on Oahu, felt that they could face an invasion force from the Japanese. However, until 18 May he kept the Army air command in Hawaii on the alert for a possible carrier attack on Oahu.[22]

Chapter 2
Midway

Midway is a 2.4 square mile atoll in the North Pacific Ocean roughly equal distance between North America and East Asia. A coral reef encircles the three small islands which make up the atoll; Sand Island, Eastern Island, and a very small Spit Island, which sit between the two. It is part of the Hawaiian Ridge-Emperor Seamounts chain and is located 1140 miles north, northeast of Oahu.

The Hawaiian Ridge-Emperor Seamounts chain extends some 3700 hundred miles from the "Big Island" of Hawaii to the Aleutian Trench off Alaska. The eight Hawaiian Islands themselves are a very small part of the chain and are the youngest islands in the immense, mostly submarine mountain chain composed of more than 80 volcanoes. The second tallest mountain and volcano in the world is located in this chain on the Island of Hawaii, the big island. The volcano and mountain Mauna Kea; when you measure the bases of mountain islands that are below sea level, it reaches 13,802 above sea level but 33,474 feet from the Pacific Ocean floor.

The length of the Hawaiian Ridge segment alone, from the Big Island (Hawaii) northwest to Midway Island is about equal to the distance from Washington, DC to Denver, Colorado (1615miles) [1]

Captain N.C. Brooks of the Hawaiian Bark Gamba, discovered the uninhabited small atoll of Midway on 5 July 1859, claiming it for America, and named it Middlebrook Islands. In 1867 it became the first offshore island annexed by the United States government and named Midway Atoll. [2]

In January 1903, President Theodore Roosevelt placed the small atoll under the control of the United States Navy. The American company Commercial Pacific Cable sent workers to Midway in 1903 to work on efforts to lay a trans-Pacific telegraph cable. In response to complaints from these cable workers about Japanese poachers and squatters, the United States Navy opened a radio station there in 1903 and 21 Marines came between 1904 and 1908 to protect the island, radio, and cable station.

Pan American Airlines (Pan Am) had in 1927 begun overseas operations to Cuba, Mexico, Central America, the Dominican Republic, Haiti, and Puerto Rico and later into South America. Because these were port cities, Pan Am had to use aircraft that could operate from the water so-called flying boats.

In 1935, Pan Am began using the Martin M-130 flying boats built by Glenn L. Martin Company in Baltimore, Maryland for Pan American Airlines to fly from San Francisco to China. It was an all-metal aircraft with large and powerful engines that could carry the fuel and range to cross the Pacific. It could carry 36-day passengers or 18 at night. It was designed for luxury and at the luxury price. It would be an island-hopping flight with overnight stays in Honolulu, Midway, Wake, and Guam on the way to Manila and eventually to Hong Kong. The large flying boats were called the Martin Ocean Transports but they were known as the China Clippers. These flights started in 1936 with stops at Midway.

The flying boats would land in the lagoon at Midway, taxi to a floating dock for unloading. Passengers were loaded into a small power launch to the pier, from there they would ride in one of their wood station wagons, called "Woody's" and taken to the hotel Pan American had built on Sand Island located on the southern end of Midway Atoll east of the eastern channel.

The hotel was a prefabricated building with 45 guest rooms, solar-heated hot water, electric lights, screened-in porches, and formal dining room, called the Pan Am Hotel but most referred to it as the Gooneyville Lodge in honor of the many albatross birds on the islands called Gooney Birds. [3]

These Pan-American flights to Midway ended on December 8, 1941, with the start of World War Two.

The United States Navy began building an airfield on Sand Island and a submarine base in 1940. An attachment of US Marines arrived in September 1940.

Twelve hours after the Japanese attacked Pearl Harbor on Oahu; two Japanese destroyers began shelling the seaplane hangar and power plant of Sand Island of the Midway Atoll. Receiving fire from the U.S. forces on Sand Island, the Japanese destroyers retired without doing further damage. [4]

Brief of the Battle of Midway

From 4 June till 7 June 1942, perhaps the most important battle of American history and deserving to be in the top five in all of world history was fought at sea and on the island of Midway. Why does this battle not deserve a higher rating?

The goal of the Japanese Empire; who had been at war since its invasion of Manchuria in 1931 and with the United States since its surprise attack on the Island of Oahu, mainly the American Naval Forces at Pearl Harbor on 7 December 1941, was the removal American Naval Force from the Pacific area. This would allow Japanese forces freedom of movement in the Pacific without interference from the American Navy, the only force that could challenge the Japanese in their conquest of the Pacific.

In April 1942 it was hard to think that the Japanese Empire could be defeated by any power existing in the Pacific Asian area at that time. Their naval superiority over the nearest naval power, the United States was staggering. They held a far advantage in aircraft carriers before Pearl Harbor and after the Battle of Coral Sea in May of 1942 still had a ten to three advantage. In battleships, the difference was greater after the U.S. losses at Pearl Harbor.

The Japanese naval advantages were high enough for the Japanese Combined Fleet Staff to approve a plan to expand their influence further to the eastern part of the Pacific. Even before the Doolittle bombing raid in March 1942, the Japanese had their mindset increasing their presence throughout the Pacific but the Doolittle attack added to the approval to increase their defense east. Being aware that the U.S. Congress had passed a "Two Ocean Navy" bill, the Japanese knew the U.S. was building carriers, battleships, cruisers, destroyers, and submarines at a fast pace. If the Japanese wanted to create this safety net and get the United States out of the war in the Pacific, they had to do it now.[5]

When Admiral Yamamoto presented his plan for Midway, the Aleutians, and other distant bases, the Japanese Combined Fleet Staff overrode each objection one by one but on 16 April, the Fleet Staff approved the Midway/ Aleutian operation but only after the attack against Fiji and Samoa was conducted.

The operational objectives for the Japanese at Midway were two-fold. First was conquering the Midway Atolls and establishing an advanced airbase from which they could make early detections of enemy forces westward from the Hawaiian Islands. The second and the more important of the two, was to draw out the remaining forces of the United States Navy from Pearl Harbor and destroy them in a decisive battle. The Japanese knew that the U.S. Navy carriers were not at Pearl on 7 December and had to be destroyed if they had any chance of controlling the Pacific.

The Japanese operational plan for Midway was the capturing of Midway before meeting the U.S. aircraft carriers. Admiral Yamamoto was under the assumption that the US carrier Yorktown had been sunk at the Battle of the Coral Sea and the American Navy had only two carriers at Pearl Harbor. His plan was built around his belief that the American Navy would send their carriers north when they learned of the Japanese attacks on the Aleutians. With his forces lying in wait near Midway he could make a decisive surprise attack and destroy the carriers and control the Pacific. His plan for a surprise attack may have worked if it had not been that American cryptanalysts had broken the Japanese codes.

Although the Japanese had won a big victory at Oahu on 7 December with their carriers, they were still a battleship navy. Their attack on Midway was built around their battleships. This was evident in how they deployed their forces around Midway. Admiral Yamamoto Main Force with his main battleships was to be 600 miles northwest of Midway. The Guard Force; which was part of the Main Force, was to be 500 miles north of Yamamoto group. The four carriers under Vice Admiral Nagumo's command were to be 300 miles east of Admiral Yamamoto's force providing a screen for him. The Second Carrier Strike Force; part of the Northern Force, once it had attacked the Aleutians would proceed 300 miles east of the Guard Force.[6]

As the end of April approached, the Japanese Combined Fleet Staff approved the Midway/Aleutian plan pushing it ahead of the Fiji/Samoa operation. They set the date for early June.

Admiral Yamamoto's plan called for a feint toward the islands in Alaska followed by the attack on Midway. Because Midway was in the defense scope of the American Naval Fleet at Pearl, Admiral Yamamoto expected the U.S. Pacific Fleet in Hawaii to respond to both attacks and to bring their two carriers to the action; that Yamamoto thought were now at Pearl Harbor. His forces would be hiding to the west and when the U.S. forces appeared, he would attack, destroying them. Thinking his plan would work, he couldn't see the

Americans able to respond with enough naval forces for at least a year. That gave the Japanese their defense bases in the eastern Pacific along the 180th parallel. This would make the Japanese a positive threat to Hawaii with bases on Wake, the Johnston Atoll, and Marcus Islands, providing ample warning of any future threat from the United States.

Yamamoto requested from the Combined Fleet Staff over 200 ships to complete these two attacks. His request included 8 carriers, 11 battleships, 22 cruisers, 65 destroyers, 21 submarines, and approximately700 aircraft.[7]

In March 1942 the Japanese Fourth Fleet using seaplanes from the Marshall Islands with refueling stop by a submarine in the French Frigate Shoals made an armed reconnaissance flight over Oahu. No damage was done but this flight did create the idea for the Americans that Hawaii may be an invasion potential for the Japanese.

In May, U.S. code breakers read a message that the Japanese Fourth Fleet had requested navigation charts for several areas including those around Honolulu and the Aleutians. This gave the United States Naval Command the indication that Oahu may be a target. Admiral Nimitz recalled Admiral Halsey to Hawaii and concluded that the Japanese would attack Midway and raid Oahu the first part of June. Admiral Nimitz knew that losing Midway to the Japanese would have been a very serious threat because they could easily take Hawaii and threaten the west coast of the United States. He also speculated that Japanese seaplane bombing raid on Oahu would not occur until a full moon, which would be the end of May.[8]

On 27 May, a message was intercepted that indicated a future deployment schedule for a unit of heavy bombers from Misawa Air based at Kisarazu in the Chiba Prefecture of Japan. To depart from Wake Island in three stages beginning 1 June and ending 3 June. They would be in the range of Midway and if the Japanese occupied Midway, these bombers could be used against Hawaii. [9]

When the Japanese fleet was ready for Midway instead of eight carriers, they had only four, 17 escort vessels, 229 aircraft, and 17 seaplanes. The rest were committed to the Aleutians or too far away to be of support.[10]

Now that the crippled Yorktown; fresh from the battle of Coral Sea, had arrived at Pearl, Nimitz had the ship repaired in record time, allowing the United States Navy able to get 3 carriers and 22 escorts vessels to sea toward

Midway along with 234 aircraft on carriers and 110 aircraft at Midway, plus several submarines on the morning of 4 June.[11]

Before the battle, the Japanese had analyzed the situation at Midway and reported the following:

The situation in the Midway Area

Midway acts as a sentry for Hawaii. Its importance was further enhanced after the loss of Wake and it was apparent that the enemy was expediting the reinforcing of its defensive installations, its airbase facilities, and other military installations as well as the personnel.

- *An estimate of existing conditions there were as follows:*

(a) *Air strength:*
    Recco. Flying Boats 2 squadrons.
    Army Bombers 1 squadron.
    Fighters 1 squadron.
    The above-estimated strength could be doubled in an emergency.

(b) *Strict Air Patrols were maintained both day and night to the West to a distance of about 600 miles. About three fighters covered the Island at all times.*

(c) *Some surface vessels patrolled the area and some submarines were active to the West.*

(d) *Of the enemy's carriers, the Ranger was apparently in the Atlantic. According to some prisoners' statements, Lexington had been sunk. There were others, however, who claimed that she was under repair on the West Coast.*

(e) *The Enterprise and the Hornet were placed in the Pacific, but we could get no reliable information as to the whereabouts of the Wasp.*

(f) *About six auxiliary carriers had been completed and there were indications that about half of this number were in the Pacific. However, they were known to be inferior in speed and could not be effectively employed for positive action.*

(g) *Air strength in the Hawaii area was estimated to be as follows:*
    Flying Boats About 60.
    Bombers About 100.

Fighters About 200.

These could be used for the speedy reinforcement of Midway.

(h) *Enemy surface units in the Hawaii area were estimated to be in about the strength noted below. It was likely that these units would sortie in the event of an attack on Midway.*

     Aircraft Carriers 2 to 3.

     Special Carriers 2 to 3.

     Battleships 2.

     Type A Cruisers 4 to 5.

     Type B Cruisers 3 to 4.

     Light Cruisers 4.

     Destroyers About 30.

     Submarines 25.

(i) *Shore Defense Installations on Midway.*

Large numbers of various types of level and high angle large-caliber guns, as well as high angle machine guns, had been installed. Marines had also been landed and all in all, the island was very strongly defended.

- *Mobile Force Commander's Estimate of the Situation:*

a) *Although the enemy lacks the will to fight, he will likely counter-attack if our occupation operations progress satisfactorily.*

b) *The enemy conducts air reconnaissance mainly to the West and to the South but does not maintain a strict vigil to the Northwest or the North.*

c) *The enemy's patrol radius is about 500 miles.*

d) *The enemy is not aware of our plans. (We were not discovered until early in the morning of the 5th at the earliest.)*

e) *It is not believed that the enemy has any powerful unit, with carriers as its nucleus, in the vicinity.*

f) *After attacking Midway by air and destroying the enemy's shore-based air strength to facilitate our landing operations, we would still be able to destroy any enemy task force which may choose to counter-attack.*

g) The enemy's attempt to counterattack with the use of shore-based aircraft could be neutralized by our cover fighters and AA fire.[12]

Admiral Yamamoto's battle plan for Midway was large and included eight separate forces. One was a diversionary attack on American-held islands in the Aleutian, another to occupy Midway Atoll with an invasion force of 5,000 men. Plus he expected the Americans to send out their last two carriers, which he would destroy.

Japanese Attacking Force

Yamamoto's First Carrier Strike Force consists of four carriers, the Kaga with 74 aircraft and Akagi with 60 aircraft as Carrier Division 1 and the Hiryu with 57 aircraft and Soryu with 57 aircraft as Carrier Division 2, plus two battleships, three cruisers, and 12 destroyers under the command of Vice-Admiral Chuichi Nagumo. Their mission was to attack Midway Atoll and destroy any air force including American aircraft carriers. This force would approach Midway from the northwest.

The First Fleet Main Force with Admiral Yamamoto in his flagship the battleship Yamato as an overall commander with three battleships, one light carrier, two heavy cruisers, one light cruiser, eight destroyers, and two oilers. None saw action at Midway. The light carrier of the trailing forces and Yamamoto's three battleships were unable to keep pace with the carriers of the First Carrier Strike Force of Vice Admiral Chuich Nagumo, so could not have sailed in company with them. The distance between Yamamoto and Kondo's forces and Nagumo's carriers had grave implications during the battle; the invaluable reconnaissance capability of the scout aircraft carried by the cruisers and carriers, as well as the additional antiaircraft capability of the cruisers and the other two battleships of the *Kongō*-class in the trailing forces, was unavailable to Nagumo.

This force stayed to the west to meet any threat the Americans gave from Midway and or the Aleutians.

Second Fleet, Admiral Nobutake Kondo commanding, was the invasion force-carrying, 5,000 soldiers, for the occupation of Midway. This force consists of 12 types of transport, three patrol boats, one light cruiser, ten destroyers, and one light carrier. It was a large landing force for such a small atoll as Midway. Perhaps they had Hawaii in their sight after taking Midway.

Midway Support Force with Vice Admiral Takeo Kurita in command with four heavy cruisers, two destroyers, and one oiler.

Minesweeper Group, Captain Sadatomo Miyamoto in commanding with four minesweepers, three sub chasers, two cargo ships, and one supply ship.

Japanese Sixth Fleet submarine force, under the command of Vice-Admiral Teruhisa Komatsu with ten submarines.

Eleventh Air Fleet - Shore based on the Northern Marianas Islands, Vice Admiral Nishizo Tsukahara commanding with 108 A6M Zero Fighters, 10 G4M Betty Bombers, 72 B5N2 Kate Torpedo Bombers, and 36 H6K Flying Boats.

Fifth Fleet - Northern Area Force, Vice Admiral Boshiro Hosogaya commanding assigned to the Aleutian Island attack with one heavy cruiser, two destroyers, two oilers, and three supply ships.

Second Carrier Striking Force Rear Admiral Kakui Kakuta commanding assigned to the Aleutian Island attack, with one aircraft carrier with 16 A6M2 Zero Zeke Fighters and 21 B5N2 Kate Torpedo Bombers, one aircraft carrier with 24 A6M Zero Zeke Fighter and 15 D3A1 Val Dive Bombers. Plus two Heavy cruisers, three destroyers, and one oiler.

Aleutian Support Force with Vice Admiral Shiro Takasu commanding with four Battleships, two Light Cruisers, 12 Destroyers, and two Oilers. With this force was an Invasion Force for Attu Island, under command of Rear Admiral Sentaro Omori with one Light Cruiser, four Destroyers, One Minelayer, and one Transporter with 1200 army troops. The Invasion Force for Kiska Island with two Light Cruisers, three Destroyers, three Minesweepers, two modes of transport carrying 1250 troops, two Auxiliary Cruisers which had been converted to carry materials and supply for construction. This Force had a Submarines Detachment with five Submarines and a Seaplane Tender with eight floatplanes and one Destroyer for protection of seaplane tender.[13]

The power of these Japanese forces was more than the American forces could muster and should have given the victory of the Battle of Midway to Japan.

Task Force 17, Rear Admiral Frank Fletcher commanding:

Task Force 17.5 Aircraft Carrier Yorktown with 25 F4F-4.

 Wildcat Fighters, 37 BD-3 Dive Bombers, 13 TBD-1 Torpedo Bombers.

Task Group 17.2 Cruiser Group with two Heavy Cruisers.

Task Group 17.4 Destroyer Screen with six Destroyers.

Task Force 16, Rear Admiral Raymond Spruance commanding.

Task Group 16.5 Carrier Group consisting of Carrier Enterprise with 27 FF-4 fighters, 23 Dive Bombers, 14 TBD-1 Torpedo Bombers: Carrier Hornet with 27 F4F-4 Fighters, 37 SBD-2/3 Dive Bombers, 15 TBD-1 torpedo bombers.

Light Cruiser.

Task Group 16.4 Destroyer Screen with 9 Destroyers.

Oilers Group with two Oilers and two Destroyers for escorts.

Task Group 7.1 with 12 Submarines.

Task Group 7.2 with 3 Submarines.

Task Group 7.3 with 4 submarines.

Also, there were U.S. Forces stationed on Midway Island consisting of:

Marine Aircraft Group 22 with 21 F2A-3 Fighters, 7 F4F-3A Fighters, 19 SBD-2 Dive Bombers, 17 SB2U-3 Dive Bombers.

Marine troops on Midway with 2nd Raider Battalion and 6th Defense Battalion with 1700 men and 9 PT Boats.

Navy Aircraft Units with 31 PBY-5 Patrol Aircraft, 6 TBF Torpedo Bombers.[12]

The material losses suffered by Japan at Midway were catastrophic. Four carriers, a heavy cruiser, and more than 320 planes were sent to the bottom of the Pacific. Approximately 3,000 Japanese sailors and airmen were killed, and, because the Japanese fleet left the action area in relative haste, there was little opportunity to recover survivors who might have gone into the water. The victory cost the United States one carrier and a destroyer, as well as nearly 150 aircraft—more than two-thirds of which were carrier-based. American personnel losses were relatively light; 317 sailors, airmen, and Marines from the Midway garrison were killed.

It was also the most decisive naval defeat suffered by Japan since 1592 when Korean Admiral Yi Su-shin destroyed Toyotomi Hideyoshi's invasion fleet, which was trying to invade China but was unable to conquer Korea.

As a result of the Battle of Midway, the U.S. Pacific Fleet permanently frustrated all Japanese ambitions to establish a defensive perimeter anchored east of the Marshalls. Most importantly, however, the victory exposed to U.S. Navy planners Japan's incapability to wage effective carrier warfare in the central Pacific.[14]

The Japanese had established Operation FS, which was the plan to invade and occupy Fiji, Samoa, and New Caledonia. The purpose was to cut the communication between Australia and the United States. It was to be executed in July or August 1942 after their victory at Midway. They could with Midway's secure attempt to attack Australia, Alaska, and Hawaii.

If the Japanese had won the battle at Midway; where they had the advantage, the only U.S. carrier in the Pacific was the USS Saratoga. With other carriers under construction but not available till 1943, the United States probably would not have agreed to any peace plan with Japanese.[15]

Chapter 3
Japan

Japan is a country surrounded by water with a long history of their naval forces and understanding this history may help us understand their action in World War II.

According to Japanese history recorded in the Korean Samguk Sagi, completed in 1145 and known as the oldest surviving chronicle of Korean history the country of War the earliest known name for Japan sent 100 hundred ships in 14 AD to invade the coastal area of what was known as Silla, one of the three kingdoms of Korea and the largest closest to Japan. But was driven off and not allow to land. This is the first recorded history of Japan using its naval forces.

From this early period up until the 1600 hundreds, Japan had inter exchanges with the Asia mainland by ship but when the Tokugawa shogunate ruled from 1600 to 1868 Japan entered a period of relative seclusion. During this period the advancement of naval technologies could not compete with modern navies when United States Navy arrived and forced Japan to give up its maritime restrictions in 1854.

After the end of the Tokugawa period, Japan entered the Meiji Renovation era which restored practical imperial rule to Japan bring the emperor back into power. This change was brought about through Japan's desire to compete with the other countries of the world. The emperor had been present during the Tokugawa period but not in any dominating role. The Meiji period saw rapid modernization and industrialization of Japan.

Fast growth by the Imperial Japanese Navy brought victories in the Sino-Japanese war of 1894-1895 with China and the Russo-Japanese war in 1904-1905, proved the changes the Japanese had made to their armed forces were successful. By 1920, the Imperial Japanese Navy was the third-largest in the world behind the British and American.

In 1921 a Conference for Naval Disarmament was held in Washington, D.C., and Japan was invited to attend. The conference put upper limits on principal battleships of major countries, one of which was Japan. The United States was limited to five, United Kingdom five, Japan three, France 1.67, Italy 1.67. Japan signed the agreement desiring to show good faith to the Western powers and due to financial pressure as their budget was out of balance.

Japan wanted to establish and maintain good relations with the United States as they were Japan's main source of oil. Plus as a member of the Big Five and a first-class country, Japan wanted to appear to be in favor of global peace and prosperity.

The ambassador to the United States at the conference was Kijuro Shidehara who became Minister for Foreign Affairs in 1924. He resisted the Japanese Army's push to move into China. By 1927 Shidehara was out and Japan sent troops into China. Followed in 1931 with the Manchurian Incident and Japan was now on a march across Asia and the Japanese Imperial Navy now had plans.[1]

Japanese early history had been one of isolation as listed in the Sakoku Edict of 1635, which restricted Japanese from traveling aboard and not allowing Europeans into Japan. Only Chinese and Dutch were allowed into the country.

The Tokugawa Shogunate; the feudal military government of Japan that ruled during the Edo period from 1600 to 1868, considered Catholicism a major threat, particularly in Southern Japan. This was one of several reasons for isolation including the desire of the rulers to maintain control of power without outside influence. The rulers of Japan were concerned about foreign influence and its effect on their control.[2]

The edict of 1635 was issued by the shogunate; the rulers of Japan at that time, to the officials administering the port at Nagasaki, the busies of all Japanese ports, and the site of most of Japan's foreign contacts at that time.[3]

The details of the Edit of 1635 were:

1. Japanese ships are strictly forbidden to leave for foreign countries.
2. 2. No Japanese is permitted to go abroad. If there is anyone who attempts to do so secretly, he must be executed. The ship so involved

must be impounded and its owner arrested, and the matter must be reported to the higher authority.

3.   If any Japanese returns from overseas after residing there, he must be put to death.

4.   If there is any place where the teachings of the (Catholic) priests are practiced, the two of you must order a thorough investigation.

5.   Any informer revealing the whereabouts of the followers of the priests must be rewarded accordingly. If anyone reveals the whereabouts of a high-ranking priest, he must be given one hundred pieces of silver. For those of lower ranks, depending on the deed, the reward must be set accordingly.

6.   If a foreign ship has an objection (to the measures adopted) and it becomes necessary to report the matter to Edo (modern Tokyo), you may ask the Omura domain the region surrounding Nagasaki) to provide ships to guard the foreign ship.

7.   If there are any Southern Barbarians (Westerners) who propagate the teachings of the priests, or otherwise commit crimes, they may be incarcerated in the prison.

8.   All incoming ships must be carefully searched for the followers of the priests.

9.   No single trading city shall be permitted to purchase all the merchandise brought by foreign ships.

10.   Samurai are not permitted to purchase any goods originating from foreign ships directly from Chinese merchants in Nagasaki.

11.   After a list of merchandise brought by foreign ships is sent to Edo, as before you may order that commercial dealings may take place without waiting for a reply from Edo.

12.   After settling the price, all white yarns (raw silk) brought by foreign ships shall be allocated to the five trading cities (Kyoto, Edo, Osaka, Sakai, and Nagasaki) and other quarters as stipulated.

13.   After settling the price of white yarns, other merchandise (brought by foreign ships) may be traded freely between the (licensed) dealers. However, because Chinese ships are small and cannot bring large consignments, you may issue orders of sale at your discretion. Additionally, payment for goods purchased must be made within twenty days after the price is set.

14. The date of departure homeward of foreign ships shall not be later than the twentieth day of the ninth month. Any ships arriving in Japan later than usual shall depart within fifty days of their arrival. As to the departure of Chinese ships, you may use your discretion to order their departure after the departure of the Portuguese ships.

15. The goods brought by foreign ships which remained unsold may not be deposited or accepted for deposit.

16. The arrival in Nagasaki of representatives of the five trading cities shall not be later than the fifth day of the seventh month. Anyone arriving later than that date shall lose the quota assigned to his city.

17. Ships arriving in Hirado (a small island off the Japanese coast, near Nagasaki) must sell their raw silk at the price set in Nagasaki and are not permitted to engage in business transactions until after the price is established in Nagasaki. You are hereby required to act under the Provisions set above. It is so ordered.[4]

The United States Navy sent several missions to Japan during the 1830s from their Far Eastern squadron based in Guangzhou (Canton), China. In each case, the Japanese did not allow them to land.

U.S. Navy Commodore James Biddle on July 20, 1846, sailed into the mouth of Edo Bay (present-day Tokyo Bay) with the USS Columbus and the USS Vincennes, in an attempt to open trade with the Japanese but was not successful.[5] While on an expedition to Canton China, Navy Captain James Glynn learned that 15 American sailors had been shipwrecked from a whaling boat on the coast of Japan and were being held by the Japanese. The commodore of the East India Squadron ordered Captain James Glynn to proceed to Nagasaki and free the sailors. Captain Glynn enter the bay on April 17, 1849, and demanded the release of the sailors or threatened intervention of the United States. With help from the Dutch, the sailors were turned over to him on 26 April.[6]

Captain Glynn advised Congress to open trade negotiations with Japan, leading to the Navy Commodore Perry's trip in 1853.

On 8 July 1953, Navy Commodore Matthew Perry; traveling with a letter from President Millard Fillmore, entered the forbidden waters of Edo Bay; present-day Tokyo Bay. The city of Edo had about one million people, making it one of the greatest urban centers of the world and unknown to the outside world.

The Japanese had experienced something about the Americans from a Japanese youth who at the age of 14 had been shipwrecked while fishing off the coast of Japan and had been rescued by an American vessel and brought to the United States. His name was Nakahama Manjiro, known as John, the name given to him by his American rescuers. He lived in Farhaven, Massachusetts for three years, sailed on an American whaler, and even went on the gold rush to California in 1849. He returned to Japan in 1852 and was questioned about his experience in America. He had high praise for the American people as upright and generous. He remarked about the technological progress including railways, steamships, and telegraph. He helped prepare a drawing of a paddle-wheel steamboat and a train. When Commodore Perry arrived, John Manjiro became an interpreter for the Shogunate.

As Commodore Perry's naval vessels entered the bay, his force consisted of two coal-powered steamers towing two sailing sloops with their sail secured. The two steamers were powered by coal and blowing black smoke; not familiar with coal-fired steamers, the Japanese people called them "black ships of evil men."

The president's letter was addressed to the Emperor of Japan. The Americans were not aware that the Japanese Emperor was just a figurehead and the real power rest with the Tokugawa Shogunate. This was a military dictatorship, founded by Tokugawa Ieyasu, who came to power as the last Shogunate in the 1600s ruling Japan for over 250 years.

Commodore Perry's mission was to complete an agreement with the Japanese Government for the protection of stranded or shipwrecked American sailors and to open one or more ports for supplies and refueling of American vessels. Although the treaty was not a commercial treaty and it didn't guarantee the right to trade with Japan, it did contain a favored nation clause that all future concessions that Japan would grant to other countries would also be granted to the United States. What the treaty allowed was future contact and trade between Japan and the United States.

Commodore Perry was ordered by the Japanese to leave but refused and sent word that unless the Japanese sent an official delegate to receive the document he had from his president, he would by force deliver them himself.

On 11 July, the Shogunate decided that simply accepting the letter from President Fillmore did not constitute a violation of Japanese sovereignty.

While anchored in the sheltered harbor near the small village of Uraga at the entrance to Edo Bay, the Commodore received word for him to move his vessels southwest to the present city of Yokosuka and was allowed to land on 14 July. Commodore Perry came ashore at 10 o'clock on the morning of 14 July 1853 with considerable pomp and force in 15 ship boats and with a 13 gun salute from his flagship the Susquehanna. He walked between a double line of heavily armed soldiers with a marine in front carrying a sword and at his side two of the largest men of his ships. In a part of the procession were two large black stewards, bigger than any other individual. The 250 sailors and marines were carrying all kinds of weapons, a show of force with some the Japanese had never seen.

As the Commodore proceeded, the Marine detachment presented arms and the ship band played Hail Columbia. Commodore Perry intended it to be a show of force with respect.

To help with this mission, he brought many gifts for the emperor, including a telescope, a telegraph, and model of a steam locomotive, tea, potatoes, and a variety of liquors and wines, plus many other gifts. All intended to impress upon the Japanese the superiority of Western culture. Commodore Perry departed on 17 July for the coast of China and promised to return to receive the Japanese answer later.[7]

In early March 1854, Commodore Perry returned with nine vessels, over 100 guns, and a crew close to 1,800. The Japanese grudgingly agreed to Perry's demands, and the two sides signed the Treaty of Kanagawa on March 31, 1854. According to the terms of the treaty, Japan would protect stranded seamen and open the two ports of Shimoda and Hakodate for refueling and provisioning for American ships. Japan also gave the United States the right to appoint consuls to live in these port cities, a privilege not previously granted to foreign nations. This treaty was not a commercial treaty, and it did not guarantee the right to trade with Japan. Still, in addition to providing for distressed American ships in Japanese waters, it contained a most-favored-nation clause, so that all future concessions Japan granted to other foreign powers would also be granted to the United States. As a result, Perry's treaty provided an opening that would allow future American contact and trade with Japan.[8]

The second visit had a greater interaction and socialization between the Japanese and the Americans. Banquets were held, gifts exchanged with entertainment and the Americans spent time onshore, observing the countryside and visiting with the local Japanese people. The treaty was signed on 31 March, meeting all the U.S. governments' requests. The treaty allowed for two Japanese ports to be used to accept provisions and refuge for shipwrecked American sailors. The Japanese were reluctant to agree to an American consul but they finally agreed. Japan was now open to a global political economy.[9]

The isolation of Japan continued until 1854 a year after Commodore Matthew Perry of the United States Navy arrived in 1853 and demanded that Japan be open to trade. This visit contributed to the outlook of Japan's future because the Japanese people viewed this as American gunboat diplomacy, which meant you will trade with us or we will force you.

In the future, the Japanese government would view this visit as one that the Japanese government would have to expand their country's influence in the world to protect itself from foreign influence.[10]

Emperor

According to mythology the reign of a sole monarchy in Japan started around 660 BC and it's known that emperors have ruled Japan for over 1500 years. The emperor line passed from male to male. In 1603, the long list of Shoguns came to power and ruled Japan for the next 250 years. Although the emperor existed during the period of the shoguns his role was ceremonial.

In 1868 came the restoration of the emperor Meiji to Japan. The military government of the Tokugawa Shogunate was replaced by the young Emperor Meiji, bring power to the Imperial house once again. His long reign from 1868 to 1912 brought about an era of major changes in economic, social, and politics in Japan. His new government wanted to be able to stand equal with Western Powers. They began to become more in line with western moderation as railroads, banking, telegraph lines installed between major cities. The emperor worn western clothes which ushered in trends in western clothing and architecture was promoted by the new powers. In 1871 a national army was formed and followed by a universal conscription law.[11]

After successful wars with China in 1894-95 Japan took Formosa and with their victory over Russia in 1904-05 gave control of the southern tip of Manchuria.

In 1905 after the Japanese victory over the Russians, President Theodore Roosevelt sent Secretary of War, William Howard Taft to Japan. A non-written agreement between the United States and Japan was discussed where the Unites States did not have any difficulty with Japan being the protectorate of Korea and Japan had no interest in the Philippines where the United States had acquired after the war with Spain in 1898. This agreement gave Japan insurance that the United States would not interfere with the Japanese going into Korea which they did in 1910.[12]

Japan joined the Allied Powers in World War I and was awarded the former German islands north of the equator in the Pacific, the Mariana, Caroline, and the Marshall Islands, and later sections of China and French-controlled sections of Indo-China. In1931 according to the sections they had been awarded in China, Japan moved into Manchuria; the northeastern part of China north of Korea.

Hirohito assumed the throne of the Empire of Japan in December 1926 upon the death of his father. He was the nation's highest spiritual authority and commander-in-chief of the armed forces. The Japanese economy was plunging and the power of the military was increasing. The emperor fired the prime minister in 1929 and the next prime minister was shot and killed and on 15 May 1932 the prime minister of Japan, Inukai Tsuyoshi was attacked by eleven naval cadets at his home, shot and killed, upset about a treaty limiting the number of Japanese warships. This was followed by another failed coup attempt on 26 February 1936 to strengthen the power of the military that militarism should dominate the political and social life of the nation and that the strength of the military is the strength of the nation.[13]

At this point, almost all prime ministers came from the Japanese military. Political unrest increased in 1935 and 1936, over 1,400 soldiers mutinied in Tokyo, seizing the army ministry and murdering several high-ranking politicians.

The Japanese navy wanted to expand south into the South Pacific and south-east Asia areas where vital resources were available for the Japanese Empire, while the Japanese army wanted to move northward. These moves were brought on by the idea that their economy was deadlocked. They had a problem with the rapidly expanding population, with a shortage of raw materials and the division of the world into economic powers from which they were not included.

The attempts of the Japanese leaders to integrate their economics into a liberal world order led to frustration when the depression of the early 1930s hit the world and western powers placed trade barriers on Japan to protect their colonial markets.

Konoe Fumimaro had become prime minister of Japan in June 1937. His cabinet fell in January 1939 but in July 1941 he formed another cabinet and assumed duties of prime minister again but in October he resigned over difference with his Minister of War, Tojo's Hideki. Fumimaro wanted to reform his government, namely the demilitarization of its politics. But the Japanese military had acquired a lot of power and was now calling the shots.[14]

In September 1940, Japan entered into the Tripartite Pack with Germany and Italy. This agreement was created as a defense alliance between these countries and was created to keep the United States from entering the conflict. It increased tension between Japan and the United States. The military powers of Japan had been misled by their own experience with the short wars of victory with China and Russian and belief that Allied weakness in Southeast Asia and American isolation would mean a short war if one occurred.

To understand Japan's aggression during the 1900s one had to consider the Japanese belief that they are descendants of the gods, that their emperor is divine, and that they have a heaven-inspired mission to rule the world.

Why did the leaders of Japan act aggressive is thought to be tied to four ideas:

1. The Japanese believe that their nation is superior to all others and that it has a special mission to dominate and rule the rest of mankind.
2. The Japanese armed forces enjoy a special position that gives them practical control of the government.
3. Japan is located at the center of the rich Asiatic-Pacific area and had the strongest and most successful army and navy in Asia.
4. The Japanese were dissatisfied with their economic condition. The working classes had a low standard of living, and big business demanded more raw materials and more markets which could be

exploited without meeting European and American competition. Japan was less rich in resources than the United States, Great Britain, and the USSR. Also, high tariffs in the United States and other countries barred Japanese goods from some of the world markets.

Japanese Prime Minister Fumimaro Konoe in the summer of 1941 ordered the Minister of Education of Japan to write a "Bible of the Japanese People" under the title The Way of the Followers or Subject's Way and distributed it to all schools in Japan.

It had several themes, one of which was as follows:

"The Imperial Family is the fountain source of the Japanese nation and national and private life issue from this. The way of the subject is to be loyal to the Emperor in disregard of self, thereby supporting the Imperial Throne co-extensive with the Heavens and the Earth."

Another theme was that "the country was contaminated by perverted thinking and our sacred duty is to clean this and to return to the virtuous customs of our ancestors. It is by working with harmony and cooperation and making manifest our national dignity that the Heavenly Spirits of our Ancestors should be obeyed in a dutiful manner, which, by working in harmony with others, is for the greater glory of the Throne."[15]

Adding to the frustration that the Japanese government had, was when the United States Senate passed the Immigration Quota Act of 1924, which part of denied immigration to Japanese and other countries. This Act was attacked in Japanese news as stated in the Japan Times and Mail, April 19, 1924:

"The Senate Declaration of War"

"There is no denying that the adoption by the American Senate of the exclusion amendment to the Immigration bill has given a shock to the whole Japanese race such as never before been felt…The Senate has passed, with an almost overwhelming majority, an amendment that they know is a most humiliating one to the Japanese race. And the events cut the Japanese deep, and one that will hurt and rankle for generations and generations."[16]

The United States government was not happy when Japan invaded Manchuria in 1931. The United States responded with a note sent to both the Chinese and the Japanese by Secretary of State, Henry Stimson; which became known as the Stimson Doctrine, stated that the United States government would not recognize any changes made in China that would infringe on American treaty rights in the area and that an open door policy must be maintained.

The American government did not like what they saw occurring in northeast China with the Japanese incursions and the rise of Japanese militarism in that area. The United States had a longstanding friendship with China but they did not see any vital interest in China worth going to war with Japan. Plus the American Government was aware that a conflict between the Chinese National Government and the rising Communist in China presented the U.S. policymakers the uncertainly of giving aid to such a divided country.

On 7 July 1937, the Japanese forces near the Marco Polo bridge at the outskirts of Beijing attempted to enter a small town to look for one of their soldiers. They were denied entry and the conflict spread further as the two countries entered what became the Sino-Japanese War. The Japanese army moved along the coast and entered the capital of Nanjing in China along the Yangtze River.

The American warship USS Panay was escorting US evacuees and three Standard Oil tankers down the Yangtze River when it was attacked by Japanese aircraft sinking the USS Panay. Japanese aircrafts machine-gunned lifeboats and survivors on the river bank, killing two American sailors and one civilian. The Japanese said the attack was unintentional and paid two million dollars in reparations. This event caused tensions to rise with the American people but the U.S. government accepted to apology and reparations and we entered an uneasy truce into 1940.[17]

Most Americans probably leaned more in favor of the Chinese over the Japanese but the United States government didn't want to cause any trouble with Japan due to the amount of trade the United States conducted with the Japanese, especially oil. The United States didn't interfere with Japan's aggression.[18]

In August 1940, Japan created the "Greater East Asia Co-Prosperity Sphere", which was to create a bloc of Asian countries led by Japan and free of western government influence. But its real intent was to establish greater security for Japan by driving Western Imperialist Powers from Asia. Its hidden intent was the quest for power for the ever-increasing Japanese Empire.[19]

President Roosevelt in 1940 and 1941 formalizing United States aid to China and tighten restrictions on Japan. This allowed the president to give China credits through the Lend-Lease program.

The Japanese knew to maintain and grow their economy they had to have certain raw materials which weren't available in mainland Japan. The critical raw materials they need were oil and rubber. Most of its oil came from the United States and rubber from British Malaya. The Japanese navy wanted to want to procure a push south attacking Dutch Indonesia to get oil and into British Malaya to control its rubber and tin production. The army would go into China to get the needed iron and coal.[20]

Needing all of these raw materials, Japan on 24 July 1941, decided to strengthen its position throughout Southeast Asia by moving into areas that had been controlled by the French for over 350 years. Japan and Germany had become allies and Germany now controlled France, the French puppet government agreed to Japan's occupation of Indo-China, which included Vietnam, Cambodia, and Laos. The Japanese now had troops less than 800 miles from American forces in the Philippines and closer to the British base in Singapore.

President Roosevelt on 26 July 1941 seized all Japanese assets in the United States, closed the Panama Canal to all Japanese traffic because of Japan's occupation of French Indo-China. The British and Dutch East Indies followed by doing the same. The results loss for Japan was 88 percent of their imported oil and three-fourths of its overseas trade.

While negotiations between the United States secretary of state and Japanese officials were ongoing in Washington, the Japanese minister of war, Hideki Tojo made it clear Japan had no intention of withdrawing from French Indo-China, Japan needs the raw materials.

Soon to be prime minister of Japan, Hideki Tojo was aware in 1927 as part of the war games at the Japanese Navy War College, one was included for their students to examine a carrier raid on US Naval Forces at Pearl Harbor. The Japanese were beginning to realize that to expand their empire throughout the Pacific they had to remove the United States Navy from Pearl Harbor.[21]

The Rise of Isoroku Yamamoto

As a lieutenant commander, Isoroku Yamamoto came to American and studied English at Harvard University from 1919 till 1921. He returned later to serve as the Japanese Naval Attaché` in Washington. While in that position, he traveled across the United States and later said, "Anyone who has seen the auto factories in Detroit and the oil fields in Texas knows that Japan lacks the national power for a naval race with America." Later he would say, "Should hostilities once break out, it would not be enough that we take Guam and the Philippines, nor even Hawaii and San Francisco. To make victory certain, we would have to march into Washington and dictate the terms of peace in the White House. I wonder if our politicians have confidence as to the outcome."[22]

Returning to Japan and rising to the captain, Yamamoto gave a lecture at the Japanese Navy War College in 1928 on carrier raids at Pearl Harbor.[23]

Yamamoto had been opposed to Japan joining Germany and Italy in the Tripartite Pact, which was signed in Berlin in September 1940. Knowing that the United States provided a large amount of the oil Japan needed, he feared rightfully knowing that the American government would cut off that supply once Japan signed that pact. He was well aware that Japan would exhaust its oil stockpile within a year and would need to find other sources.

When President Franklin Roosevelt decided to move the Pacific Fleet from San Diego to Pearl Harbor in 1940, Yamamoto took that to be a signal that the United States Navy was now in striking distance of Japan. He is reported to have said, "we are in striking distance, too. In trying to intimidate us, America has put itself in a vulnerable position. If you ask me, they're just that bit too confident."[24]

Once Japan invaded Southeast Asia seeking raw material, mainly oil, Yamamoto argued for war with the United States reasoning that once U.S. Naval Forces were attack and removed from the Pacific area, they would sue for peace. Once presented to Emperor Hirohito, the emperor adopted this view.

After Japan had raided Southeast Asia in 1940, Admiral Yamamoto privately stated he described the nature of the next war as, "As I see it, naval operations of the future will consist of capturing an island, then building an airfield in as short a time as possible within a week or so and moving up air units, using them to gain air and surface control over the next stretch of the ocean. Do you think we have the kind of industrial capacity to do that?"[25]

Admiral Yamamoto became commander of the Japanese Combined Fleet in 1939 and began to discuss an attack at Pearl Harbor in March or April 1940. He knew to be successful in the Pacific he had to get the United States to withdraw from that region and if he could put the US Navy's battleships out of action, they had a chance and where were the US battleships? at Pearl Harbor of course. But Yamamoto faced a problem, he couldn't just decide to attack Pearl Harbor, he had to get the Navy General Staff approval. The Navy General Staff made these types of decisions. Approaching the General Staff led to back and back discussions about this subject; some heated at times. On 5 November 1941, the Navy General Staff finally gave their approval for the attack on Hawaii Island of Oahu. Admiral Yamamoto started planning for the attack, which was successful on 7 December 1941.[25]

Knowing that the United States had to have some sort of answer for the Japanese attack on 7 December; Roosevelt approved the Doolittle raids on Japan's homeland in April 1942, shocking the Japanese people and showed the Japanese leaders that there were gaps in their defenses around the homeland. The Japanese military leaders with the approval of the Emperor began to study how to better expand their defense perimeter. Along with Admiral Yamamoto, other military leaders knew that the United States Navy was the primary opponent to their expansion.

Admiral Yamamoto, knowing that the US carriers were not at Pearl on 7 December, decided he had to draw the carriers out to defeat that threat, allowing Japan to proceed unopposed across the Pacific. He first studied attacking Pearl Harbor again when the carriers were there, hoping to draw them out but disregarded this idea not knowing that land-based forces had been increased that might come out to attack his fleet.

Looking over his options, he found the tiny atoll of Midway to be the ideal choice. Being a little over 1,000 miles from Pearl Harbor, it was beyond the range of aircraft from Hawaii. Plus he suspected the United States would consider it a vital outpost and would defend it. To Yamamoto that meant United States naval carriers would come out.

Now Admiral Yamamoto with the Imperial Japanese Navy had to get the Imperial Japanese Army to agree. The Imperial Army wanted to invade and occupied a couple of islands in the Aleutians, Attu, and Kiska controlled by America. To their thinking, this would put the homeland of Japan out of reach of US land-based aircraft flying across Alaska.

This phase included a plan to occupy Midway and the Aleutians to establish an outer defense line to the east and northeast of Japan. Occupation of these points was to be followed by the establishment of air coverage from these bases to a radius of 1,300 miles, a radius which included the Hawaiian Islands.

Knowing that Midway Atoll was key to the defense of Hawaii, Yamamoto hoped to draw the American fleet out so that it could be destroyed. His plan included moving east with a large force, including four carriers, while also sending a diversionary force to the Aleutians. He thought once Midway was seized, Hawaii would be invaded, forcing the U.S. to sue for peace.[24]

Admiral Yamamoto believed that the main strength of the American Navy lay in Hawaiian or Australian waters and that the attack at Midway would be a complete surprise to the Americans. Once his forces had captured Midway, he thought the remnants of the U.S. fleet would be forced to attempt its rescue. By then the Japanese would have the advantage of position as well as at least a 2:1 advantage in carriers and four to five times the number of screening vessels. At that point, Yamamoto himself would lead the combined fleet's main force, a powerful unit of seven battleships that included the two largest in the world then or since his flagship *Yamato* and her sister ship, the *Musashi.* While he would be shutting the jaws of a gigantic trap, the northern force would come from the Aleutians to cut off the U.S. line of retreat.[24]

Yamamoto called for his force of 5,000 troops to land and occupy Midway and force a possible invasion of the Hawaiian Islands now that the American Navy had been defeated in the Pacific. With this in his mind, he thought it would force the United States Government to sue for peace in the Pacific.

Interrogations of Japanese Officials after the war showed intend to land and occupy Midway with Japanese troops:

An interview with Japanese First Air Fleet CinC Vice Admiral Nagumo stated that they departed Hiroshima Bay on 27 May 1942 for Midway Island to provide air support during the planned Japanese occupation on about 6 June 1942.

Other points of interviews of Japanese captains that survived the war and were at Midway:

Q. Were there any other forces such as Support Force or Occupation Force?
A. Believe there were two other forces for occupation, but am not sure of composition or relative location.
Q. What was the mission of the Carrier Task Group?

A. To attack MIDWAY, to help occupation.

Q. When you left JAPAN what was the mission of the air fleet at MIDWAY?

A. It was to seize MIDWAY.

Q. Why didn't the occupation force and Grand Fleet continue to MIDWAY?

A. Because we could not occupy the island having lost our air attack force.

The First Air Fleet, CinC Vice Admiral NAGUMO, departed HIROSHIMA Bay on 27 May 1942 for MIDWAY Island to provide air support during the planned Japanese occupation about 6 June 1942.

Q. What was the mission of your air fleet?

A. We were to bomb MIDWAY in preparation for a landing operation to be made by transports approaching from the southwest 4-7 June 1942. [25]

As a result of this battle, the Japanese expansion to the east was stopped and Midway Island was saved as an important American outpost. To the Japanese this battle was disastrous. The loss of 4 of their finest aircraft carriers, together with 250 aircraft and some 100 of their first-line pilots deprived them of the powerful striking force with which they had achieved their conquests and with which they had planned to cut down United States efforts to counterattack. Battleships and seaplane tenders were withdrawn from the fleet for hasty conversion into carriers, but all efforts to regain what had been lost were insufficient, and from this date, the balance of power in the Pacific shifted steadily to the United States side. Because of the strategic situation at the time and the condition of United States defenses, the carrier action at Midway was perhaps the decisive battle of the war and perhaps all of American history.

We have an example of what the Japanese could have done if they had won the battle of Midway in their attack in September 1942. A Japanese floatplane launched from a submarine dropped two incendiary bombs into the Oregon forest expecting to cause massive fires. A Japanese victory at Midway most likely would have caused many attacks of various weapons on the U.S. west coast.[26]

Plus the possibility of delaying the invasion of France in 1944, as Roosevelt shifted forces from the Atlantic to the Pacific and could have brought new German secret weapons into the war.

Chapter 4
China

If the Japanese had won the battle at Midway, we would have to understand a little about China to visualize what could have occurred there with a Midway victory and the Japanese further expansion into China.

The Population of Japan was growing as it increased from 55.9 million in 1920 to 69.2 in 1935 and 73.1 in 1940. The population density in 1920 was 147 people per 56.7 sq miles to 181 in 1935 and 191 in 1940. Most of Japan is covered by mountains with Tokyo being the largest city where the population in 1920 was 2.17 million to 5.87 in 1935 and 6.78 in 1940.[1]

The growing population needed more natural resources such as iron, tin, and coal, which were not readily available locally. Food needs to be increased for items such as sugar, seafood, certain vegetables, rice, and dairy products. In 1940 a rationing system for these items was imposed. The Japanese government knew that they had to look elsewhere for these items and China was close and had many of these products.

China had been in the textile business; mainly silk, for centuries but after World War I, they increased their export of textiles and this affected Japanese textile industries. Although the depression of the 1930s had a worldwide effect, the Japanese suffered greatly by the rise of tariffs by other countries almost killed their exportation of silk, plus the Chinese lower-priced silk had a big effect on the Japanese economy and gave rise to Japan's militant nationalism.

China was having internal problems which grew worst after the Shanghai massacre of 1927. The Chinese Nationalist forces joined by certain gangs began to purge the city of Shanghai of communists. This brought the Communist Party of China to expand their efforts which led to the Central Plains War across China in 1930. From this point forward internal conflicts between the Chinese Nationalist Army and the Communist Party of China prevented from China defending against an invading Japanese army.

Manchuria in southeast China offered oil, lumber, and rubber, Japan need all of these for their fast-growing industries. Plus Manchuria was a large area and could help Japan's population problem.

Japan believed that a neutral Manchuria was important for the defense of Korea which Japan had annexed in 1910 when President Theodore Roosevelt had agreed to Japan's control of Korea in the Taft-Katsura Agreement of 1905, which Japan agreed not to interfere with the United States interest in the Philippines.

Once in Manchuria, Japan felt threaten with the successful unification of China with the rising Chinese Nationalist Party and the pressure from the Soviets in the north.

On 18 September 1931 the Kwantung Army, which controlled the puppet state in Manchuria for Japan and was the largest army group for the Imperial Japanese Army from 1919 to 1945; charged that Chinese soldiers attempted to bomb a South Manchurian Railway train. Little damage was done and the train arrived safely. But it gave a good excuse for the Kwantung Army to capture the city of Mukden and occupy all of Manchuria.

With Japan in control of Korea moving troops from Japan through Korea, which was next door to Manchuria was easy.

Although the Republic of China had been formed in 1912, its central authority had disintegrated due to the rise of regional warlords. It was not in a position to fight Japan because of Manchuria, leaving their only resource was the League of Nations. The only pressure that the League of Nations could bring was economic and with the great depression affecting the world, it wouldn't have had any effect.

Things now in Europe were on the brink with the rise of Nazism, the war in Europe had not yet started. When World War II began its' spread throughout most of the world in 1939, we can say that with the invasion of Manchuria; part of China, by Japan that World War II began in September 1931.

From 1931 to 1937, small and localized engagements occurred between Japan and China. These were referred to as incidents. The biggest of these was the Marco Polo Bridge incident in 1937. It can be said from 1937 on; Japan was in a constant war with China, referred to as the Second Sino-Japanese War.

The Chinese Eastern Railway was built by the Russian Empire from 1897 to 1902, having received a concession from the Chinese Imperial government. At the time of its construction, this railroad was the shortest route from European Russia to Russia's port of Vladivostok on the Sea of Japan.

The Russians want to build the Eastern Railway to connect their Trans-Serbian system to their port city Vladivostok. It crossed northern Manchuria and was the main railway system in Manchuria.

In 1919, the Soviet government foreign minister stated that they would return the Chinese Eastern Railway to the Chinese but the Soviets never followed through. In 1929, the Chinese Northeastern Army took control of the Railway. The Soviets responded with quick military action, moving 156,000 troops into the Manchuria border forcing the Chinese to return the railway.[2]

Japan had been interested in Manchuria for its raw material was surprised by the action of the Soviets; however, the Soviet Consul to Tokyo was able to get an agreement from Japan that the Japanese would not interfere as long as the Soviets limited their action to Northern Manchuria.

When the Japanese invaded Manchuria in 1931, the Soviets weren't strong enough in that region to resist and sold their rights to the Chinese Eastern Railway in 1935.[3]

The Chinese Communist Party had its beginning in Shanghai in 1921. The Chinese Nationalist Party had its founding in 1912 but dissolved by a coup d'état in 1913. It rose again in 1924 with help from the Soviets. The Nationalist Party didn't rise to real power till 1925 under Chiang Kai-shek. Many parts of China were controlled by local warlords, which Chiang Kai-shek ended their autonomy by 1928.[4]

By the time the Japanese invaded Manchuria, the Chinese Nationalist Party was more interested in fighting the Chinese Communist Party. In turn, the Communists were fighting the Nationalists and local warlords were creating problems in northwest China. By 1941, Japan held most of the north and eastern coast of China and Vietnam.

If the Japanese had won the battle of Midway, their expansion into China would most likely have continued and would have required more allied forces to drive them out as the United States tried to regain the Pacific and East Asia.

Chapter 5
United States

American isolationism became the theme for many in the United States during the 1930s. It reached its' peak in 1940 when influential private citizens joined a group of Congress members to form the American First Committee (AFC) and appointed Charles A. Lindbergh as its head. Lindbergh carried a lot of influence because of his fame. The specific goal of this committee was to prevent the United States from becoming involved in World War II now going on in Europe and Asia.

This Committee held a meeting on 4 September 1940 and Lindbergh told the gathering that while isolationism did not mean walling off America from contact with the rest of the world, "it does mean that the future of America will not be tied to these eternal wars in Europe. It means that American boys will not be sent across the ocean to die so that England or Germany or France or Spain may dominate the other nations."[1]

"An independent American destiny means, on the one hand, that our soldiers will not have to fight everybody in the world who prefers some other system of life to ours. On the other hand, it means that we will fight anybody and everybody who attempts to interfere with our hemisphere," Lindbergh explained.[1]

Related to the overall war effort, the AFC also opposed President Franklin Roosevelt's Lend-Lease plan to send U.S. war materials to Britain, France, China, and the Soviet Union. "The doctrine that we must enter the wars of Europe to defend America will be fatal to our nation if we follow it," said Lindbergh at the time.[1]

Having reached a peak membership of over 800,000 the AFC lost its effort when the Japanese attack Pearl Harbor on 7 December 1941. It disbanded on 11 December 1941 but in its final press release, the Committee stated that while its efforts might have prevented it, the Pearl Harbor attack made it the duty of all Americans to support the war effort to defeat Nazism and the Axis powers.[1]

After World War I, Republican Senator Gerald P. Nye of North Dakota help create isolationism when he claimed that American bankers and arms manufacturers had pushed for United States involvement in that war for their profit. The 1934 publication of the book "Merchants of Death" by H.C. Engelbrecht and F. C. Hanighen, followed by the 1935 book "War Is a Racket" by decorated Marine Corps General Smedley D. Butler both created the suspicions upon the public that wartime profiteering was why the United States was pushed into wars it had no business being involved. All of this moved many of the American public in the direction of neutrality.[2]

After World War I, the United States Government rejected membership in the League of Nations. Many members of Congress were opposed to membership thinking it would drag the United States into more European conflicts. This was a push for more isolationism within both Congress and the public.

Now in the middle of a worldwide economic depression and seeing the fast-changing events in Europe and Asia, the American public saw the need for increased attention to domestic problems and not to be involved in events in other parts of the world. During the 1930s, the League of Nations proved ineffectual in the face of growing militarism, partly due to the U.S. decision not to participate.1

During the interwar years between World War I and World War II, the United States government lacked the coordinated effort of a central intelligence agency to know what was occurring in various parts of the world. They had four different agencies collecting data. The Navy had their Office of Naval Intelligence (ONI) and the Army their Military Intelligence Division (MID), both of which collected and analyzed military and political information to support war planning and procurement, as well as security and counterintelligence. The State Department had their intelligence activity through their diplomatic corps, which provided political intelligence to support U.S. foreign policy and economic decision making. The fourth arm was the Federal Bureau of Investigation (FBI), which had principal responsibility for domestic counterintelligence and counterespionage. The Central Intelligence

Agency (CIA) had not come into existence yet, which allowed the FBI to gather bits of intelligence in Central and South America as well.

The results of four different agencies collecting intelligence was the lack of sharing their data with the other agencies. No central authority existed that could coordinate the information. The results were often duplicative collections, analysis, and reporting. Plus inter-departmental rivalries existed which limited sharing. It wasn't till the summer of 1941 that the office of Coordinator of Information; later becoming the Office of Strategic Services (OSS), was founded by President Roosevelt to solve the problem of lack of coordination between the four agencies and placed Wild Bill Donovan in charge. Now Roosevelt had one person that he trusted to solve this problem and that was Donovan.[3]

When Franklin Delano Roosevelt was elected to the office of President in 1932, his number one problem was a great depression that the country was experiencing; he had to deal with that problem first. On the back of the burner, he wanted the United States to take a more active role in international affairs. He knew he would and did run into strong isolationists in Congress, which limited his ability to get his ideas on foreign affairs to Congress.

Having been the Secretary of the Navy, Roosevelt was well aware of things going on in certain parts of the world. This knowledge; when he became president, led him to keep his eye on events occurring in Europe with the Nazis in Germany and the events occurring in Italy with Mussolini. He was displeased with the Japanese move into Manchuria in 1931, a Chinese territory, rich in minerals that Roosevelt knew the Japanese needed for their growing population. When Japan attacked China in 1937, he offered aid to China because many Americans had a strong business interest in China. His aid was limited due to neutrality laws and the strong power of the isolationist in American politics and strong outspoken individuals in the public eye such as Charles Lindbergh.

Those who supported isolationism were from all backgrounds, including conservatives, progressives, business owners, and peace activists. They were not opposed by any organized group which created a problem for Roosevelt's desire for the United States to be involved in international affairs. This began to change in 1937 when the situation in Europe was growing worst with the Nazi Party gaining more strength and with Japan now at war with China. But non-involvement in international affairs in congress did not stop even after the outbreak of war in Europe in 1939, but public opinion was shifting from total neutrality to giving limited aid to our Allies short of complete involvement which meant troops.

President Roosevelt could see the rise of the Japanese Empire in Southeast Asia and knew that Japan would become a problem but the present threat, in his opinion was the Germans in Europe. He had to somehow limit the powers of Japan by isolating them while dealing with Europe first. Working with Prime Minister Churchill, he created the Europe First strategy.

Japan knowing they needed vital resources to continue to expand their economy with their ever-growing population. They knew from China they would have access to iron, coal, soybeans, and salt. From the United States oil, from British Malaya rubber.[4]

Wanting to help China in their fight against Japan, Roosevelt formalized U.S. aid to China in 1940 giving credits to purchased war supplies. Trying to force Japan to stop its aggression into China, Roosevelt started to restrict the flow of war materials into Japan and moving toward an embargo on all militarily useful items to Japan including oil.

The British Empire had expanded beyond what the present British government could protect, the Japanese knowing this established the "Greater East Asia Co-Prosperity Sphere" in 1940-1941, which announced that Japan intended to drive all Western imperialist nations out of Asia. The Japanese government signed several pacts with Germany and Italy linking the activities in Europe with those in Asia. A neutrality pact with Russia and an agreement with Vichy France allowed the Japanese to move into Indochina, rich with many resources that Japan needed.

Roosevelt responded by putting into effect a total embargo on exports to Japan, freezing all Japanese assets in U.S. banks, and sending more supplies into China.

In January and February 1941, the United States, Britain, and Canada held a series of secret meetings in Washington, D.C. known as the ABC-1 Conference which discussed a joint strategy that their first objective was the defeat of Nazi Germany with the main effort of the U.S. military would be in the Atlantic and European areas. The second strategy was defensive action in the Far East. This agreement established the Europe First or Germany first key element of the grand strategy.

A Japanese victory at Midway could have changed Roosevelt's mind on his Europe First policy.

During the ABC-1 Conference, the British stated that their position was:

1. The European Theater is the vital theater where a decision must first be sought.
2. The general policy should therefore be to defeat Germany and Italy first, and after that, deal with Japan.
3. The security of the Far Eastern position, including Australia and New Zealand, is essential to the cohesion of the British Commonwealth and the maintenance of its war effort. Singapore is the key to the defense of these interests and its retention must be assured.

Based on this conference, the British wanted the United States Naval Forces to be deployed mainly in the Atlantic and Mediterranean. Aware of the Japanese action in the Pacific they suggested that the U.S. should only maintain a Pacific fleet large enough to prevent the Japanese from affecting the main effort in the Atlantic.[5]

President Roosevelt had appointed Joseph P. Kennedy as U.S. Ambassador to Great Britain in 1939, a decision Roosevelt would later regret. Kennedy was opposed to the United States getting involved with England in a war in Europe and was against the position of the U.S. State Department and Roosevelt in aiding Britain in the war. Roosevelt was receiving negative news from the U.S. Ambassador and want to have a trustworthy individual go to England and give him and the State Department the truth about the chances of England holding on now that France had fallen. Roosevelt knew he couldn't trust opinions from Ambassador Kennedy.

New elected Prime Minister Churchill sent retired Army Colonel William Stephenson, a Canadian millionaire, to take over the British Passport Control Officer (PCO) post in New York City. The PCO was the thinly veiled cover for the senior Secret Intelligence Service (SIS) officer in the United States and the role of this office was known to high-ranking officials in the U.S. government. While Stephenson's primary point of contact for counterintelligence and counterespionage activities in the U.S. was FBI Director J. Edgar Hoover, he was also in personal contact with Roosevelt, both directly and through associates. He was to direct all U.S.-based British Security operations and coordinated all British overseas espionage in the Western Hemisphere. Stephenson had been an old friend of William Donovan, both had serviced in World War I as pilots, Stephenson for the British and Donovan for the Americans. Churchill wants Stephenson to get the U.S. to increase its' aid to England.

During a meeting, attended by Secretary of the Navy Frank Knox, Secretary of War Harry Stimson, William Donovan, and William Stephenson, during which U.S. Navy destroyers for bases deal was discussed, Stephenson knew that the big question the U.S. had was if Britain would survive the summer. The U.S. government needed proof that their material assistance would be a sound investment, not charity. Stephenson suggested sending Donovan on an independent fact-finding mission to Great Britain.[6]

William Stephenson informed British Central Security Service (CSS) headquarters that Donovan was arriving by steamer and that his evaluation of the British war effort would be key to getting the U.S. destroyers deal and closer cooperation with the United States. It was interesting to note that Ambassador Kennedy was not informed but his Naval Attaché Navy Captain Allan Kirk; a personal friend of Donovan, and staff were advised. [7]

Donovan visited London between 15 July 1940 and 4 August 1940. His mission was to observe and assess England's chance of surviving the war now that France had fallen. Thinking that the British would put their best foot forward for Donovan, Captain Kirk saw to that. Donovan was given unrestricted access to military facilities, intelligence organizations, and factories. He also talked to English people of all classes to see their will to fight. He met with King George VI, Prime Minister Churchill, various government ministers, industrialists, and labor leaders. He was taken to see Britain's coastal defenses, radar installations, fighter-interceptor bases, and was given full briefings by Director of Naval Intelligence (DNI) Godfrey, head of the MI6 Sir Stewart Menzies, and others on a range of intelligence matters to include the functioning of the SIS, British propaganda and Special Operation Executive activities, and their highly successful counterintelligence activities.[8]

Donovan returned to America on 8 August 1940 and reported to Roosevelt, Stimson, and Knox that the British were well worth the investment in American resources as they had the will to survive.

His positive endorsement of Britain's chances allowed Roosevelt and others in the U.S. Government to put aside the fear that Great Britain would fall. Roosevelt knew that the information he was getting from his Ambassador Kennedy was not correct. Washington knew that Kennedy had met secretly with German diplomats and was known for his anti-Semitic remarks. Roosevelt wanted to keep Kennedy out of the loop. This was the turning point in the relationship between Great Britain and the United States.

Relations between the Director of Naval Intelligence and the U.S. naval attaché office became much closer after Donovan's visit, but several other factors aided in creating a closer relationship between the two organizations between August and October of 1940. These exchanges orchestrated by the British tied the two countries closer together although the threat of war to the United States was but a few months away.[9]

The Americans agreed with the British that Germany was the main enemy and a threat to the world and that the principal effort of both nations should be made to defeat Germany. Many thought as stated in the United States-British Staff Conversations Report, (ABC-1), pp 1492 as follows:

"Since Germany is the predominant member of the Axis Powers, the Atlantic and European area is considered to be the decisive theatre. The principal United States Military effort will be exerted in that theatre."

In December 1941, President Roosevelt declared that, in the event of a German victory, "all of us in the Americas would be living at the point of a gun a gun loaded with explosive bullets, economic as well as military."

Roosevelt was good about keeping his ear to what the American people were saying about the war in Europe. He knew that academics, politicians, journalists, and military officers viewed Hitler's Germany as the preeminent threat to the ideological and economic integrity of the United States. It helped him understand the need for a Europe First policy. On purpose, he used this strategy to get it officially and unofficially fed it into his speeches, talks with members of Congress, and saw that it was in use by the press and other articles.

From the period May 1940 to May 1941, American military officers and civilians within the Roosevelt administration created, shaped, and integrated the Europe First policy.[10]

A new event happened on 7 December 1941 which changed everything. The Japanese in a surprise attack on the Hawaii Island of Oahu including the U.S. Naval Station at Pearl Harbor brought destruction to almost all of the United States Navy battleships.

Prime Minister Winston Churchill; shortly after the attack by the Japanese on Pearl Harbor, headed to Washington to meet with President Roosevelt in what became known as the Arcadia Conference. His purpose was to confirm the Europe First strategy, which Roosevelt did while holding action against Japan. Even after the Japanese attack on Oahu, Roosevelt re-affirmed Europe's First policy and he made plans to ship more resources to the Pacific to hold off the Japanese. It wasn't till 1944 that the U.S. became to push more to the Europe First strategy.

The Europe First strategy wasn't completely accepted by the U.S. Military. It created some division between the Navy and Army. The Navy Plan Orange was established after World War I but undated several times emphasizing the Pacific and war with Japan. The Army after World War I had shifted away from the Pacific toward Europe. The United States Navy Fleet Admiral Ernst King said the Pacific effort deserved 30% of the U.S. resources but only getting about 15%. King working with Army General Douglas MacArthur was able to get more resources into the Pacific War.

In April 1939, the joint military planners considered the problem that action by the Axis powers in both the Atlantic and Pacific areas could create a situation of a two-front war. They re-examine the Orange plan and viewed the plan as "unsound in general and wholly inapplicable to present conditions." A new plan was needed to provide for a position of readiness along the west coast of the United States and a strategy for Alaska, Hawaii, and Panama. The military had to assume that the Japanese may attempt attacks anywhere in the eastern part of the Pacific.

Shortly after this plan was submitted, the Joint Planning Committee reported it was unable to reach an agreement with the military. The Army members not knowing what would be happening in Europe would not agree to an offensive operation in the Pacific beyond those essential to the west coast, Alaska, Hawaii, and Panama.[11]

United States Army and Navy officials are in rather a general agreement that Great Britain cannot encompass the defeat of Germany unless the United States provides that nation with direct military assistance.

One of the few polls conducted during the war was taken in February 1943 which showed that 53% of Americans said that Japan was the chief enemy of the U.S. while only 34% chose Germany. During the first six months of the war in1941, the U.S. Army sent over 300,000 soldiers to the Pacific area and only 100,000 to Europe. Of these, three divisions went to Australia and New Zealand. Because Britain and the United States could not agree on a timetable for an invasion of Germany in France, the U.S. was able to assign more men to the fight against Japan.

At the end of December 1943, the United States had deployed 1,873,023 men, 7,857 aircraft, and 713 warships against the Japanese. Against Germany, the United States had 1,810,367 men, 8,870 aircraft, and 515 warships. As plans were being made for the invasion of France in 1944, the United States began to move more resources into the Europe effort, making Europe First a reality instead of a stated objective.

The American victory at the Battle of Midway reinforced the Europe First policy but if the Japanese had won the Battle of Midway, the effort to move more U.S. resources to Europe may have not been possible as the focus had to be on protecting Hawaii and the U.S. west coast and may have changed our Europe First approach.

By the end of the war, the United States Army had 47 divisions in Europe and 21 divisions and six Marine Corp divisions in the Pacific. 78% of army and air power was in Europe versus 22% in the Pacific against Japan. After Germany was to be defeated, 15 of the 47 European divisions would be transferred to the Pacific.

Although it had been the strategy of Europe First after the ABC-1 Conference in January and February 1941, and many scholars disagree but the final figures show that the United States' efforts in Europe and the Pacific were close to equal.[12] Of course a new winner in the Battle at Midway would have changed these statistics.

Chapter 6
Great Britain

The surprising attack by the Japanese Empire on 7 December 1941 against the island of Oahu in Hawaii and President Roosevelt's declaration of war against Japan on 8 December 1941, called for Prime Minister of England, Winston Churchill to visit Washington, DC on 22 December 1941. Although Germany had declared war on the United States on 11 December, Mr. Churchill knew that Americans would now want their government to go all in to defeat the Japanese. He wanted to make sure that President Roosevelt would stand by their policy of Europe First, which was adopted in March 1941 at the ABC-1 Conference in Washington, DC.

Churchill was concerned about how U.S. policy would affect the war in Europe now that the United States was at war with Japan. Would the U.S. now divert its main focus from Europe to the Pacific? If this was to happen, Churchill worried that Hitler might crush Russia and then would be unstoppable in Europe. Roosevelt assured him that the U.S. would remain with the Europe First policy. Roosevelt must have thought that if Hitler invades England and conquered it, the last point for an invasion of Europe by allied forces would be lost.

President Roosevelt assured Prime Minister Churchill that the U.S. would adopt a holding position against the Japanese until the war in Europe against the Axis powers was won.

Mr. Churchill knew now that France had fallen to the Germans in June 1940 that Great Britain had to have American forces with them to survive this war. Churchill also had his eye on the survival of the British Empire which had many of its life colonies, dominions, protectorates, mandates, and other territories under their rule and now was threatened by Japan.

To understand Mr. Churchill's desire to save the British Empire and the need for the Europe First policy, we have to look at the history of the British Empire to understand this move toward the Europe First policy.

The start of the British Empire goes to the reign of Queen Elizabeth I, who was on the throne from November 1558 till March 1603. After Christopher Columbus made his trip to the new world in1492, European countries began stretching their legs on overseas adventures seeking treasuries. Queen Elizabeth, I entered England in this quest when she granted a charter to Sir Humphrey Gilbert in 1578 to plant an English colony in America. After arriving in present-day Newfoundland and remaining for some days, he headed back to England but was lost at sea. His half-brother, Walter Raleigh received a patent from the queen and established an English settlement on the coast in what would become North Carolina.

Another major act that Queen Elizabeth I did to help start the British Empire was the granting of a charter to the East India Company in 1600. The East India Company establish a presence on the Island of Java and Surat in India. This company went to established colonies in the Caribbean and other parts of Asia.[1]

The British Navy grew under King Henry III in the 1200s but it developed into a major defense for Queen Elizabeth I when it together with the weather defeated the Spanish Armada in 1588. Perhaps the high point of her reign. She made naval strength a high priority of her rule. She was aided by great sea captains such as John Hawkins and Francis Drake, who extended the British Empire around the globe. The British came up with new ideas for building ships and tactics for using them in battle.

The new technology of that time allowed for the full-rigged sailing ship. This allowed for ships to sail faster, maneuver better and carry more and heavier guns. This changed the tactic for the battle at sea while in the previous action, the captains had to ram and get close enough to board, now they could standoff and shell their enemy ships.[2]

From 1603 until the Act of Union in 1707, Scotland had their Royal Scottish Navy and England their English Royal Navy. Although they were two separate navies, they operated together. With the Act of 1707, they merged and became the Royal Navy.

The British Empire began to expand in the 1600s with the territories of Plymouth and Salem in North America, Jamaica, and Barbados in the

Caribbean, and Guiana in South America. In 1610, Capers Cove in Newfoundland, Canada was established by a charter from King James I as the first English colony in Canada. Moving into the next century, the British Empire added more areas in Africa, India, Newfoundland, Gibraltar, and the Island of Menorca in the Mediterranean. After losing the American colonies in the 1700s, the British Empire added Australia, New Zealand, and other islands in the Pacific. In the 1800s the islands of Java, followed by Singapore, Malacca in Malaysia and Burma. After World War I, the British Empire added Palestine, Transjordan, Iraq, plus parts of Cameroon in British West Africa, Togoland, and Tanganyika both in Africa. Plus other areas were added when the Union of South Africa gained South West Africa and Australia gained New Guinea, New Zealand gained Western Samoa.[3]

During the 19th century, the population of Britain at home was increasing rapidly, mostly in the urban areas causing social and economic problems. The British government began to look outside of England for sources of raw materials and new markets for British goods. They expanded into Egypt and South Africa while Canada, Australia, and New Zealand became self-governing dominions.

After the battle of Waterloo against French forces in 1815, the British Navy became the superior navy in the world. With peace now in Europe for the first time in years, the British Navy in effect became the global policeman.[4]

In the 19th and 20th centuries, the British Empire was larger than any other empire in the history of the world and it was said, "the empire upon which the sun never sets," was often used to describe the British Empire. Its Empire was so large that the sun always shined on some part of the Empire. By 1913, the British Empire held sway over 412 million people, 23% of the world population. It covered 13,700,000 square miles or 24% of the Earth's total land area.

As the 20th century dawned, the United States and Germany were beginning to challenge Britain's economic power. This brought economic and military tension between Britain and Germany and perhaps was one of many reasons for World War I. Before 1914, Germany had the most prosperous economy of all of Europe.

After the defeat of Napoleon, eight countries sent delegates to Vienna to work out an agreement for the reorganizing of Europe and would decide the future of all the conquered territories. This act called the Congress of Vienna was signed on 9 June 1815. One of its major faults was it didn't consider the nationality of the people who lived in those areas and what language was spoken. These territories stayed in place for 40 years.

On 27 July 1905, Kaiser Wilhelm II of Germany sent a letter to Russian Tsar Nicholas II stating the start of a new leaf in the history of the world. Wilhelm was referring to the recently signed Treaty of Bjorko between Russia and Germany. This treaty neutralized the alliance between Russia and France, thereby freeing Germany in case of having a war on two fronts in Europe.

It was Wilhelm's way of creating a continental league including France against the British Empire and leaving Germany the master of the European continent. This act would in many ways contribute to World War I.[5]

Starting in about 1908, various governments began to annex regions across what was established in the Congress of Vienna taking in the populations that spoke their language. This caused other signers of the Congress of Vienna to form alliances with others. When Archduke Franz Ferdinand and his wife were assassinated on 28 June 1914, the seeds for war were already in place. It only needed something to kick it off.

Terrorists from Serbia were coming into parts of Austria-Hungary and attacking citizens. Knowing that Russia was closely tied to Serbia and Austria-Hungary needed help if Russia would enter into an attack on Serbia the Austria-Hungary government source help from Germany. Unable to get Serbia to stop the terrorist, Austria-Hungary declared war on Serbia on 28 July 1914. Hearing that Russia was mobilizing, Germany declared war on Russia on 1 August. Germany then attacks Russia's allies France through Belgium, violating Belgian neutrality which by treaty brought Britain into the war against Germany, starting World War I.

This war to end all wars may have dragged on for several more years if the United States Senate didn't vote on 4 April 1917 to declare war on Germany. President Woodrow Wilson had appeared before a joint session of Congress on April 2, 1917, to ask for such a declaration due to Germany's unrestricted submarine warfare to the Atlantic and Mediterranean. On 26 June 1918, the first American troops land in France under the command of General John Pershing.[6]

Germany and her allies surrendered on 11 November 1918 and World War I ended. The peace treaty; which became known as the Treaty of Versailles; was drafted between January and May 1919 had several faults which would surface in about 20 years. It was drafted too fast, didn't allow Germany to participate, burdened Germany with the responsibility and high cost of the war. The British people as well as its' government felt this was unfair to the Germans and would not allow them back into the family of nations of Europe. France having suffered heavily opposed any attempt by the British to soften the penalty against the German people. This created a split between the French and the British and pushed more into a period of isolation.

What effect would this have on the British Empire as the world moved into the 1930s and the worldwide depression hit? Problems were beginning to pop up around the world as Japan faced pressure at home with overpopulation and scarcity of raw materials and the rise of the Nazi party in Germany. It became apparent that Britain would no longer be able to support such a widespread empire.

Adolf Hitler's rise to power in Germany on 30 January 1933 created little interest in England. Most in Britain knew very little about him and felted that he wouldn't be in a position of power long. This all changed in January 1935 when the area of Saar River Basin; which the Treaty of Versailles had awarded to France, voted to return to German control. This vote brought out one major problem with the treaty in 1919 that ended World War I created, failure to consider the language and customs of people in the territories that were divided under that treaty. Most of the people in the Saar River Basin were Germans.

President Theodore Roosevelt sending of his Secretary of War, William Howard Taft to Japan in 1905 gave Korea to Japan, indicating that the United States would not interfere with Japan becoming the protectorate of Korea and Japan would have no interest in the Philippians which the United States had acquired as a result of their victory over Spain in the Spanish-American War of 1898. Japan formally annexed Korea in 1910 giving it easy access to next-door China.[7]

With Japan's move into China in 1931 and showing interest in other parts of that country; Britain although not a strong friend of China began to reach out to China knowing that they may need China's help as Japan move into that part of the world could affect the British Empire.

Although Britain had to be concerned about the many parts of her Empire, she faced greater problems closer to home as Hitler's rise to power in Germany began to sounded alarms about a possible threat in Europe.

Because of the vote in the Saar River Basin in 1935, Hitler introduced the military conscription and the creation of the Luftwaffe, both violating the Treaty of Versailles of 1919. England, France, and Italy met in April 1935 to discuss how to hold Germany to the disarmament of the Treaty of Versailles. The result of this meeting was the appeasement of Hitler.

To make matters worse for Britain, the Italians under their fascist dictator Benito Mussolini invaded the independent country of Ethiopia in East Africa in 1935. Although Ethiopia had not been part of the British Empire, England did send forces to join Ethiopian rebels to drive the Italians out by 1941. This move further weakens the far-reaching arm of the British Empire.

Unchecked, Hitler continued to expand as he entered the Rhineland in 1936. The Rhineland was a strip of Germany that borders France, Belgium, and the Netherlands. It was set up in the treaty of Versailles in 1919 to create a demilitarized zone to increase the security of these three countries from Germany in the future.[8]

In early 1938, Nazis in the country of Austria; south of Munich, Germany tried to take control of the government of Austria and join Nazi Germany. On 11 March the Austrian Chancellor resigned and pleaded with the Austrian military not to resist the Germans' invasion. The next day, Hitler joined his troops as they entered Austria to a welcoming crowd and proclaimed Austria as a federal state of Germany.[9]

In September 1938, the new prime minister of England Neville Chamberlain met in Munich with Hilter and a representative from France in what became the Munich Agreement. This agreement allowed Germany to occupy Sudetenland part of Czechoslovakia which was Germany speaking. Hitler preached that German-speaking people belonged to Germany.

Both the French and British were desperate to avert another world war. Many young men in both countries had died in the First World War and the people wanted their government to do all they could to divert another conflict. The British Empire; where the sun never sets, was overstretched and couldn't afford another war. Appeasement was raising its head again.[10]

Hitlers' march across Europe continued without any resistance by England or France. President Roosevelt had his eye and ear on what was going on in Europe but the Congress of the United States and the American people didn't want any involvement with conflicts in Europe. Hitler's army moved and occupied the rest of Czechoslovakia on 15 March 1939. England seeing that

Poland could be in Hitlers' eye next, signed a military agreement with Poland on 31 March 1939. The only country that was able to defend Poland was Russia but the Polish government would not allow Russian troops to enter their country. Knowing Poland's position with Russia, Hitler did on 23 August signed an agreement with Russia for a nonaggression pact. On 1 September 1939, Hitler invaded Poland, and Britain and France declared war on Germany on 3 September.

When Hitler attacked Poland in 1939, England began to send troops to the French Belgium border and by September 1939, they had about 158,000 men in that area. Hitler's army had rolled across France and in such a move forced the remaining British forces toward the small town of Dunkirk in northern France near the Belgian and French border on the shores of the North Sea. Sitting on the Strait of Dover, just 21 miles across the English Channel some 338,000 British troops and allied forces retreated into this small town where they fought from 26 May till 6 June as all boats possible from England crossed the channel time and time again to evacuated them to England. This ended the British Expeditionary Force in France with a cost of about 68,000 men.[11]

A major event occurred on 3 September 1939; that the British people would come to appreciate when Winston Churchill was appointed First Lord of the Admiralty. This event started Churchill on his rise to be the one person who would lead Britain successfully through World War II. He had held this position in World War I but was deeply moved as he assumed the office again as reported by the Third Sea Lord Bruce Fraser remembering: "As he took the First Lord's chair in the famous Board Room, Churchill was filled with emotion. To a few words of welcome from the First Sea Lord (Sir Dudley Pound)," he replied by saying what a privilege and honor it was to be again in that chair, that there were many difficulties together we would overcome. He surveyed critically each of us in turn and then, adding he would see us all, later on, he adjourned the meeting, 'Gentlemen,' he said, "to your tasks and duties."[12]

The British Navy had established a blockade of Germany but with Hitler's German fast race across Europe, Hitler was able to get around the blockade and lucky for Churchill, as just becoming First Lord of the Admiralty didn't suffer for this naval loss.

Starting on 10 May 1940, in just six weeks Germany rolled across France conquered it, Belgium, Netherlands, and Luxembourg. France fell in just 38 days. On 9 and 10 April, German forces overran Demark and Norway, which completed their northern flank and destroyed the naval blockade of Germany. This ended Germany 's land operations on the western front.

Hitler's success in his Norwegian campaign caused the fall of the Chamberlain government and the selection of Winston Churchill as prime minister on 10 May. Perhaps the British didn't know it but they now had a leader that would lead them to victory.

Now that British forces had been driven back across the English Channel and France had surrendered, in Hitlers' mind the war was over, leave was granted, the Luftwaffe shifted to other details. Hitler counted on the British Government to compromise on a peace plan which he was ready to offer but the British now had a leader in Winston Churchill who would not give in to any of Hitlers' demands and would not allow any peace compromise.

After England non respond to Hitlers' peace compromise, Hitler had two choices, one was to lay siege to England, to wear it down physically and psychologically through limited military action; like the V-1 rocket attacks, and through political and propaganda warfare, which was included.[13]

On 16 July 1940 Adolf Hitler issued Directive Number 16. It read, "As England, despite the hopelessness of her military position, has so far shown herself unwilling to come to any compromise, I have decided to begin to prepare for, and if necessary to carry out, an invasion of England…and if necessary the island will be occupied." [13]

No positive answer from Britain on a compromised peace plan, Hitler had now conquered all of France and sitting on the channel looking over at England waited. Would he now try to conquer England? But the new Prime Minister of the British Empire, Winston Churchill had other ideas. Knowing that France had fallen, the new prime minister announced on the radio that Britain would fight on alone.

Many in Nazi Germany admired the British, they had a strong military tradition and the British Empire stretched around the globe. The British Navy was the best the world had ever seen. But many in Germany disliked the British because of their part in the Treaty of Versailles which ended World War I and had humiliated Germany. Plus Britain was an ally with France and Hitler was seeking revenge.

The new prime minister; Winston Churchill, addressed Parliament on 18 June 1940 referring to the collapse of France and the statement the commander of Allied armies in France, had said. "What General Maxime Weygand called the Battle of France is over. I expect that the Battle of Britain is about to begin…Let us, therefore, brace ourselves to our duties, and so bear ourselves that if the British Empire and its Commonwealth last for a thousand years, men will still say, This was their finest hour."[14]

It became very clear that the new Prime Minister Winston Churchill wanted to keep and protect the British Empire throughout the world.

Britain began to prepare their defenses and stockpiling ammunition for a German invasion. They didn't see an invasion at the earliest until mid-September. They thought that weather might hinder an invasion at that time.

Finally, on 16 July 1940, Hitler ordered preparation for an invasion of England and named the plan Operation Sea Lion and that his forces be ready by mid-August. On this date, Hitler signed the Fuhrer Directive No. 16 giving the go-ahead for the invasion.[15]

The Germans had planned on 41 divisions be ready by 25 August to cross the English Channel and two airborne divisions. The plan was for the landings to be along the south coast of England between Ramsgate on the east coast, 78 miles east of London, and the county of Dorset on the southwest, 123 miles south of London.

Once the Germans had taken England, Hitler's plans called for all males between the teens and mid-40s to be moved across the channel to slave labor camps and putting women to work in men's jobs in England. Hitler was very fond of ex-King Edward VIII who gave up the throne for his American wife. They had visited Hitler before the war. He wanted to place Edward on the British throne.

Hitler's plan called for the use of what was called the Einsatzgruppen, a SS death squad that they had used on the Eastern Front to murder people. Hitler planned to send them into roundup and kill those that were subversive to German rule.

Now that Prime Minister Churchill had rejected peace with Germany he knew that Britain stood alone against 2,000 miles of hostile coastline. He had to convince President Roosevelt to help Britain if not entering the war at least provide vital equipment and supplies.

Lucky for the Prime Minister his British Security chief to the United States, William Stephenson had sent a message informing British Central Security Service headquarters that a special envoy for the United States, William

Donovan would be arriving by steamer and that his evaluation of the British war effort would be key to getting United States assistance for their war effort.

On 8 August 1940, Hitler issued his Fuhrer Directive No. 17- For The Conduct of Air and Sea Warfare Against England. It contained the necessary conditions for the final conquests of England by use of intensifying air and sea warfare against the English homeland. He instructed the German Air Force to overpower the English Air Force in the shortest possible time. The attacks are to be directed primarily against flying units, their ground installations, and their supply organizations, and also their aircraft industry and manufacturing antiaircraft equipment.[16]

In other words, the Battle for Britain had begun but two major problems stood in the way of Hitler's plan for the invasion of England, the Germans army had never undertaken such a large invasion by sea. The German army had never trained for such an event or even contemplated it. How about the landing craft needed for such a task, where could they be obtained. The army would have to have time to practice embarking and disembarking. Many German generals didn't like the risk their forces would face crossing the Channel.

The second problem was the British Navy, the largest in the world and the German admirals knew their forces could not protect such an invasion force unless the British navy could be controlled. Hitler knew that the success of his invasion would rest with the ability of the Luftwaffe to control the skies over the channel and England. With his aircraft bombing the British navy, he was convinced the invasion force would cross the channel and land on English soil.

Hitler called on his man in charge of the Luftwaffe, Marshall Hermann Goring. Goring was convinced his air force could drive the Royal Air Force out of the skies. Hitler decided that he would hold his army's invasion force and his navy until the Luftwaffe controlled the skies. The plan invasion was now postponed till mid-September.

Starting on 10 July and continuing through early August, German bombers attacked British shipping, ports, and convoys as V-1 rockets brought destruction to parts of London.

On 13 August Hitler launched his main offensive air attack called Adlerangriff (Eagle Attack) against English air bases, aircraft factories, and radar stations in southeastern England. The overall object was to wear down the air defenses of Britain.

The Germans had based their aircraft in an arc from Norway in the north to Cherbourg on the north coast of France. They had prepared for the air attack about 1300 bombers and dive bombers, plus another 900 single-engine and 300 twin-engine fighters. The British had about 300 front-line fighters divided into four defense sectors, covering main parts of England including Wales and Scotland. The Britons figured that with their forced spread out into four sections, as German aircraft were detected they could launch aircraft from several sectors to attack.

One important defense item that the British had was their advanced radar system. The most operational and advanced system in the world, called Chain Home. This radar system prevented the element of surprise by the Luftwaffe as most income flights were detected while they were over the English Channel.[17]

The RAF used their heavily armed Hawker Hurricanes against the incoming bombers and their fast Supermarine Spitfire against the German fighters protecting the bombers. The German bombers were the lightly armed twin-engine Junkers Ju88, these bombers proved the best against the British in the Battle of Britain because of their high speed when diving to escape the British fighters. The other German bomber used was the Heinkel He-111; it had a light bomb load capacity and was not as effective against daylight raids because they were easy targets for the British fighters. The German fighter was the Messerschmitt Bf109 single engine but its limited flying range of about 410 miles provided little protection for the German bombers.[16]

By August 1940, the Germans had lost over 600 aircraft to the RAF 260. On 20 August, Prime Minister Churchill speaking before Parliament said, "Never in the field of human conflict was so much owed by so many to so few."[18]

On 19 September Hitler ordered that all German shipping be dispersed and on 12 October he announced that Operation Sea Lion was off for the winter. The Battle for Britain was over and the British had won but the bombing by the Luftwaffe would continue including rocket attacks.

After President Roosevelt won an unprecedented third term in November 1940, his Chief of Naval Operations, Admiral Harold R. Stark met with the president privately and warned Roosevelt that the failure of the United States to assist Britain against Nazi Germany would most serious lead to England's defeat and give Germany domination over all of Europe, Africa, and the

Middle East. Admiral Stark argued that American aid to Britain should include U.S. participation in the war in Europe and North Africa. Admiral Stark stressed that Germany should be the United States' top priority regardless of any threat from Japan.

Based on Admiral Stark advice, Roosevelt formally designated it as Plan D. It was called Plan D because it followed the numbering in Stark's formal memorandum to the President.[19]

On 6 January 1941, President Roosevelt gave his State of the Union Address to Congress in which he presented his lend-lease plan for England. Harry Hopkins, a close and personal friend of President Roosevelt had been a strong supporter of the lend-lease plan and pushed it with members of congress. He had urged Roosevelt to use the navy to protect convoys going across the Atlantic before the United States declared war on Germany.

Roosevelt decided to send Harry Hopkins as his emissary to Britain to see the conditions of England and their ability to hang on against the German attacks. Hopkins was unknown to Churchill and others in his government but Churchill's aide Brendan Bracken called Hopkins "the most important American visitor to this country we have ever had."[20]

Churchill spent a lot of time with Hopkins and in his memoirs, Churchill stated that Hopkins was a "natural leader of men who had a flaming soul."[21]

Hopkins dealt with priorities, production, political problems with allies and had more power than the entire State Department.

On Saturday 8 February 1941, Harry Hopkins started his long journey back to the United States and on Monday 10 March, William Averell Harriman; on record as a supporter of American intervention in the war in Europe, left on a mission for Roosevelt as his defense expediter. He was to see how Britain was doing and to see if Churchill got all he needed and that he was getting the best use of the American aid now that Roosevelt had gotten the Lend-Lease Bill through congress.

Based on Admiral Stark's advice, Roosevelt formally designated it as Plan D, which was the military-strategic war Plan Rainbow 5. Rainbow 5 was one of five plans that the U.S. Military had adopted during what was occurring in Europe in 1938-39 to deal with certain events with given countries. Rainbow 5 dealt with Germany, Japan, and Italy. The plan stated that if the United States became engaged in war with these three powers that U.S. military power would be used against Germany and Italy first.

Rainbow 5 required that the United States would adopt a defensive position in the Pacific behind a line between Hawaii and Alaska. Rainbow 5 was the abandoning everything west of Hawaii, including the Philippines and Australia to the Japanese.

Supporting the President's plan was U.S. Army Chief of Staff, General George C. Marshall who agreed that America would join Britain in pursuing a "Germany First" or "Europe First" strategy if the United States entered the war on Britain's side.[20]

"That those threats to the American way of life and the interests of the United States in Europe, Latin America, and the Far East against which threats the huge new defense program of this country is directed all stem, in the last analysis from the power of Nazi Germany."[22]

"The Atlantic world, unless it destroys itself, will remain infinitely superior in vigor and inventive power to the too prolific and not too well-nourished Orientals."[23]

"Since Germany is the predominant member of the Axis Powers, the Atlantic and European area is considered to be the decisive theatre. The principal United States Military effort will be exerted in that theatre."[24]

Chapter 7
The Atlantic Fleet

The surprise attack by the Japanese at Pearl Harbor damaged six United States battleships and sunk two, removing them from any action in the Pacific until replacements or repairs could be made. Eight battleships were in the Atlantic Fleet on 7 December 1941.

If the Japanese had sunk the last three United States carriers in the Pacific at the Battle of Midway, the Navy's presence in the Pacific would cease to exist. Faced with pressure from many sources, including those who feared an attack by the Japanese on the west coast of the United States, President Roosevelt would have been forced to send various navy ships to the Pacific from the Atlantic Fleet, chief among these would be aircrafts carriers including CL-4 Ranger, CV-5 Yorktown, CV-7 Wasp, CV-8 Hornet, and AVG-1 Long Island, a small escort carrier, all assigned to the Atlantic Fleet.

All United States navy ships on the east coast of America were assigned to the Atlantic Fleet under the command of a four-star admiral located at Naval Station Norfolk, Virginia. The Atlantic Fleet along with the Pacific Fleet had been established by President Theodore Roosevelt in1906.[1]

At the time of the Japanese attack on Oahu in December 1941, the Atlantic Fleet was larger than the Pacific because they were involved in protecting convoys crossing the Atlantic to England. It consisted of the aircraft carriers CL-4 Ranger returning to Norfolk from the Caribbean, CV-5 Yorktown at Norfolk, CV-7 Wasp in Bermuda, CV-8 Hornet fitting out of Norfolk, AVG-1 Long Island, an escort carrier at Norfolk.

Eight battleships, BB-33 Arkansas in Maine, BB-34 New York in Newfoundland, BB-35 Texas in Maine, BB-40 New Mexico at Norfolk, BB-41 Mississippi in Iceland, BB-42 Idaho in Iceland, BB-55 North Carolina in Maine, BB-56 Washington in the Gulf of Mexico.

Plus there were five CA heavy cruisers, seven CL light cruisers, 98 DD destroyers, 61 SS submarines spread through the Atlantic and Caribbean.[2]

The Atlantic Fleet was heavily involved in the Battle of the Atlantic and needed many of their ships to conduct that mission.

England declared war on Germany in September 1939 and need vital supplies that the United States and Canada could supply. The only problem for the United States was their neutrality. The first escorted merchant ship convoy crossing the Atlantic sailed in September 1939.

The fall of France in 1940 gave the Germans U-boats bases on the Atlantic coast. With the sinking of the German battleship Bismarck in May 1941, the Germans increased their U-boat attacks in the Atlantic and the Mediterranean operating in groups called wolf packs. The Germans increased their attacks on Atlantic convoys.

As the United States continued its neutrality, during December 1940 Roosevelt introduced a new policy allowing the United States to lend not sell goods to England. This increased the number of ships sailing across the Atlantic to the British Isles. Wolf packs attack increased and many merchant ships were sunk. The loss was so heavy that Prime Minister Winston Churchill coined the phrase "Battle of the Atlantic" in March 1941.[3]

The Atlantic is a big ocean covering over 41 million square miles. After losing many ships, the British reintroduced the convoy system that they had used in World War I, although this system had been used by the Spanish in the 16th century to protect their ships sailing to and from the new world. Because of the size of the Atlantic Ocean, it was difficult for the Germans to find convoys but their U-boats were successful in sinking over 1550 ships during World War II.

Convoys were normally several columns of ships with up to five ships in each column, forming a big box that could contain up to 60 ships.[4]

Early in the war, German U-boats took a heavy toll on merchant shipping as the Allies struggled to find effective ways to combat the enemy threat. Between 1939 and 1942, the Germans increased the number of U-boats from 30 to 300 and developed effective hunting techniques like using groups of submarines, called wolf packs, to attack convoys. The use of wolf packs was successful in the early stages of the war having sunk over 454,000 tons of cargo in June of 1941 alone. Between January and July 1942, close to 400 Allied ships were lost while German U-boats' losses were seven. The Allies were losing merchant ships faster than they could replace them.

Allies began to use aircraft to protect the convoys but at that stage in the war, the Allies' airplanes didn't have the range to protect the convoys to their destination. They reached a point where the escorting aircraft had to turn back due to fuel. This area became known as the "Black Pit", the area where the German wolf packs would wait to attack. Only after the Allies had aircraft with a longer range would the safety of the convoys increase.[5]

The United States Navy introduced the sea-based Airborne Antisubmarine Warfare in 1940 in the North Atlantic with the creation of the escort carrier to protect the convoys in the mid-Atlantic. It provided an anti-air platform of TBF Avenger torpedo dive bomber and F4F fighter aircraft from these small carriers. During the war, they were credited with sinking 42 German submarines and helping to keep the North Atlantic free of attacks from German submarines.

As the war moved into 1943 and 1944, credit for the success of these anti-sub missions was due to British ULTRA interception of German radio traffic on their submarine location and with the HF/DF fixes on submarine transmissions.

Due to the need to surface to recharge their batteries, the German submarines could be detected by radar or spotted visually. To overcome this problem the Germans in 1944 introduced the first snorkel to their existing U-boats and in 1945 developed the Type XXI and XXXIII both had the ability of high speeds underwater and to operate largely independent of the need to surface for longer periods.

If the Japanese had won the Battle of Midway, President Roosevelt may have had to move some of the small escort carriers to protect the west coast, not making them available for the Atlantic Fleet convoy protection.

The Battle of the Atlantic became the longest battle of World War II, starting in September 1939 and ending with the surrender of Germany in May 1945. Roosevelt was convinced; regardless of the pressure he was getting from certain members of Congress, from the press and some from the public, that he saw the Nazis as an evil threat to civilization and he would do all he could to help the English until the United States would join the war. The United States was in what was called an undeclared naval war against Nazi Germany and became most intense between September and December 1941.[6]

The year 1942 was a tough year of ships at sea as over 1,000 allied ships were sunk by German U-boats and German aircraft in the Atlantic and off the East Coast of the United States. During the entire war, Germany lost close to 800 of the 1,100 U-boats produced, resulting in 28,000 of the U-boats sailors killed of the 40,000 who served. German submarine duty was one of great risk.[7]

It appears that with all the reinforcement that had been sent to Hawaii after the attack by the Japanese on the island of Oahu in December 1941, that it would have been difficult for the Japanese to get enough troops in the area for a successful attack on Oahu after their victory at Midway. As the Japanese would have controlled the sea with the defeat of the U.S. Navy carriers at Midway, they could move some of their carriers off the coast of Hawaii and controlled all shipping between the main land of the U.S. They also could have invaded and controlled any of the other Hawaii islands with the 5,000 soldiers they had taken to Midway. Controlling the sea would offer the Japanese many options including an interception of any shipment from the United States mainland to Hawaii which could lead to starving the population of Oahu, opposing any effort by the U.S. or Hawaiian force to retake any island in the Hawaiian chain that the Japanese had occupied, plus with their aircraft carriers, the Japanese would have controlled the air in and around Hawaii.

President Roosevelt would have had no choice but to move forces from the Atlantic Fleet and troops from the mainland to the Pacific area.

In June 1942, President Roosevelt had the following ships available in the Atlantic Fleet that he could send to the Pacific, the aircraft carriers USS Ranger CV-4, USS Wasp CV-7, and the escort carrier USS Long Island, CVE-1. The USS Hornet CV-8 had been assigned to the Atlantic Fleet but was selected to be the carrier to take Doolittle 16-B-25 aircraft on the Doolittle Tokyo raid.

The USS Hornet arrived in San Diego on 20 March 1942. She moved to Pier 1 at NAS Alameda where 16 B25 aircraft were loaded on 1 April for the Doolittle raid on Tokyo. The Hornet continued west to join Admiral Halsey on the USS Enterprise as Task Force 16. The Doolittle raid was now underway.

The USS Hornet was already in the Pacific and was part of the Battle of Midway. If the Japanese had won the Battle of Midway, the USS Hornet would have most likely been sunk.

The Ranger CV-4 was the first aircraft carrier designed and built from the keel up. It was small, just 730 feet long, and weighing only about 15,000 tons.

The best speed was a little over 29 knots and too slow for the fast carriers that the Japanese had in the Pacific. It remained in the Atlantic because the navy thought it couldn't keep up with the Japanese carriers. She had been used in April and May 1942 ferrying aircraft off the coast of Africa. In June 1942 she was off Newfoundland but could have been available for the west coast.

The USS Wasp CV-7 was assigned to the Atlantic Fleet and had joined the British Fleet in April 1942 to ferry British fighters to Malta. She was available to Roosevelt and on the last day of the Battle of Midway, June 6th, she sailed as part of Task Force 37 with the battleship USS North Carolina from Naval Station Norfolk. She was escorted by the heavily armored cruiser USS Quincy, the light cruiser San Juan, and six destroyers. They traveled through the Panama Canal on 10 June on the way to the Pacific.

The light carrier USS Long Island CVE-1 departed Norfolk on 10 May 1942 and reached San Francisco on 5 June where she joined Admiral Pye's four battleships to provide air cover to defend the west coast of the United States. Being already in the Pacific, east of Hawaii Island, the USS Long Island could have been available to Roosevelt to defend attacks by the Japanese on Pearl Harbor or the west coast. However, Japanese carriers that could have survived the Japanese victory at Midway would have been larger and faster than Long Island.

Other ships in the Atlantic Fleet were five battleships with BB34 New York, BB33 Arkansas, and BB35 Texas in Division five and BB56 Washington and BB55 North Carolina in Division Six. There were five heavy cruisers in Division Seven, four light cruisers in Division Two, four light cruisers in Division Eight, and four light cruisers in Division Ten. Also, there were 81 destroyers and 68 submarines. The new USS Hornet CV-12 was under construction but wouldn't be complete till 1943.[8]

If the Japanese had won the battle at Midway with all of her four carriers intact and the three US carriers destroyed, they would have held a strategic advantage over the USS Ranger, a small air wing due to the size of the ship and its slow speed.

The USS Long Island, a light carrier with only 19 Wildcat fighters and 12 Dauntless dive bombers on board would not have been a match for the firepower of the Japanese carriers.

The USS Wasp was the only full-size aircraft carrier that carried a full air wing that could offer firepower against the Japanese carriers. But it was just one ship and it wouldn't be till mid-1943 that other aircraft carriers would be available to the Pacific Fleet.

It was clear that a victory for the Japanese Navy at Midway in June 1942 would have alternated the course of the war in both the Pacific and in Europe.

Once the United States declared war and Japan, Germany made a declaration of war against the U.S. on 8 December 1941, followed by the United States declaring war against Nazi Germany on 11 December.

The U.S. was now in a war in both Europe and the Pacific, plus it had agreed with Great Britain that the United States would abide by the Europe First Policy. A victory by the Japanese at Midway would have caused problems for President from the American people plus congress for maintaining the Europe First policy.

If the Japanese controlled the waters and sky of the Pacific Ocean, the people in Hawaii and along the west coast of California, Oregon, and Washington State would demand the president move military force to protect their areas.

North Atlantic convoy of 24 ships steaming south of Newfoundland, Canada, on 28 July 1942. From Naval History and Heritage Command - 80-G-21187

Chapter 8
Germany

The Treaty of Versailles officially ended the Great War or The War to End All Wars in June 1919. One observer of that treaty; Marshall Ferdinand Foch of the French Army, stood at the table and declared it wasn't a sense of peace at all, but a mere twenty-year armistice.[1]

Germany was punished heavily, it had to disarm, hand over territory, and pay steep reparations to the victorious powers, essentially footing the bill for the most expensive war ever fought. Its economy teetered on the brink for the next 20 years. The country suffered runaway inflation in 1923, recovered slowly in the mid-1920s as the rest of the world prosperous then plunged into absolute economic collapse with the onset of the Great Depression. Unemployment soared into the 35% range, and once again, unscrupulous politicos like Hitler were willing to stoke the rage. By 1932, his Nazi Party was the largest in Germany.[2]

On 30 January 1933, Germany's President Paul von Hindenburg appointed Adolf Hitler Chancellor of Germany. In March 1933, Hitler came to power when the Reichstag (Imperial Diet or Parliament) adopted the Enabling Act of 1933, which allowed the Reichstag; which Hitler controlled, to issue laws governing the country without parliament approval. This paved the way for complete control of Germany by the Nazi party with Hitler in charge.

Hitler's book, Mein Kampf (My Struggle) when published in two volumes in 1925 and 1927, it became the bible for National Socialism in Germany's Third Reich. The major theme was the superiority of the Aryan race, Hitler's plan for Aryan world rule. By 1939 it has sold 5,200,000 copies and had been translated into 11 languages.[3]

After the fall of France to German forces in 1939, Germans' Naval Grand Admiral Erich Raeder met with Hitler on 21 May 1940, bring up the topic of an invasion of England. This operation was named Operation Sea Lion and was planned for around 25 August.

In September 1940 Hitler ordered that all German shipping be dispersed and on 12 October he announced that Operation Sea Lion was off for the winter. His attack on England was on hold.

On 22 June 1941, Hitler made one of his greatest mistakes of the war; he launched the largest invasion force in history named Operation Barbarossa against Russia. Over three million German troops attack Russia in three parallel offensives. Operation Barbarossa was key to Hitler's plans for world domination.

Although Germany had signed a non-invasion pact with Russia in 1939, the Russian invasion of Rumania in 1940, threaten Hitler's oil supply from the Balkan. Because Germany had no local source of oil and was now only get some from their synthetic fuel. Hitler immediately moved his forces into Poland to counter the move that Russia had done.

If anyone in Russia had taken the time to read Hitler's book, Mein Kampf, he stated his desire for Russia in 1925. Stalin now the dictator of Russia had been warned by many in his own country and by Winston Churchill that Hitler would attack, his force was unprepared. Because the Red Army was disorganized, Hitler's army moved 300 miles into Russia in the next few days. Hitler had now had opened a second front, which he would live to regret.

The German forces in Operation Barbarossa attack to capture Stalingrad began in August 1942 and they were defeat by Russian forces in February 1943. The defeat proved that Operation Barbarossa was poorly strategized due to Hitler's overconfidence.

Due to the pressure Russia was now getting from the Germans on their eastern front, Joseph Stalin began to push Britain and the United States to open a second front in northwest Europe along the French coast to relieve pressure on the Russians. Roosevelt and Churchill agreed that the only way to defeat Germany was a massive invasion of mainland Europe. But they couldn't agree where and when.[4]

The United States was now involved in a big war with the Japanese in the Pacific and Roosevelt informed Churchill in March of 1942 that due to pressure in the Pacific and the lack of ships available for a European invasion that an invasion in 1942 was not possible.[5]

The Battle of Midway occurred in June 1942 and Roosevelt's conversation with Churchill about the U.S. not able to invade Europe in 1942 due to war in the Pacific was in March 1942. If the Japanese had won the Battle at Midway then Roosevelt's thoughts of invading Europe would have had been put on the backburner as his attention would have to be to shift forces to protect the west coast and Hawaii.

Roosevelt and Churchill both knew that they had to do something to relieve the pressure the Russians were getting from the Germans on the eastern front. Without some relief, Roosevelt and Churchill were concerned that Stalin may reach a peace treaty with Hitler.

In March 1942, Roosevelt sent his closest foreign adviser, Harry Hopkins, and General George Marshall to meet with Churchill to discuss ways to defeat Germany. General Marshall agreed with Churchill that the United States and Britain should work together to defeat the Axis powers, focusing on Germany first then Japan.

Their discussions resulted in a proposal to seize ports along the French northwest coast and launched a major invasion in the spring of 1943 under the name Operation Sledgehammer. This operation would be mainly an American one that would land troops on the Cotentin Peninsula of northern France, which was occupied by the Germans, taking the key city of Cherbourg until a full invasion could be launched. Due to many factors include those from the British military advisers that this plan was premature, it was canceled.

Once again Roosevelt and Churchill looked for ways that could help Russia, get American troops in the war and relieve pressure on British forces. They decided on an invasion of French North Africa and named it Operation Torch. Operation Torch was launched on 8 November 1942. After three years of the Germans and Italians being on the offensive, American forces were now in the battle against the Germans for the first time since World War I. Together with the British, they were now putting pressure on the Germans and Italians and relieving some of the pressure on the Russians.[6]

Because some French forces; called Vichy French, were aligned with Germany, the Allies didn't know how the French would respond to such an attack. Soon finding that most French resistance was low, Operation Torch became a successful operation. It did give some relief to the Russians and gave the British and Americans more time to plan an attack on the western coast of German-occupied France.

Although Churchill knew that Roosevelt was hindered by the Japanese in the Pacific and not ready to launch a massive invasion of France, Churchill favored attacking through Italy. It proved how important was the American victory at Midway. If the Japanese had won at Midway, any American operation in Europe would have to take a backseat to the U.S. turning their attention to stopping the Japanese in the Pacific. After the attack on Pearl Harbor, U.S. naval and army units had re-enforced Oahu to prevent an invasion but if the Japanese controlled the Pacific Ocean much of the U.S. naval force would have had to be moved from the Atlantic Fleet to the Pacific.

Always trying to please Stalin and as the Allies were working together on Operation Overlord; the plan for the invasion of the western coast of France, Churchill wrote Stalin in January 1944 to ensure him that they were going full blast for Overlord.

Chapter 9
German Weapons

This chapter discusses the weapons Germany had before going into
World War II

Following the plan in his Mein Kampf, Hitler knew to make the German race the superior one in the world he had to have the power to conquer and to rule. He knew that this could only be brought about by striking fast, which he did with his Blitzkrieg lightning war and having new weapons that other countries did not possess or had any knowledge of. After gaining power Hitler appointed Albert Speer as Minister of Armaments and War Production. Under Speers' authority lay the design, testing, and production of the new German super weapons.

In 1938, German scientists working on new weapons discovered nuclear fission. The Nazis organized a special scientific unit headed by Werner Karl Heisenberg; a well-known quantum physicist and directed him to develop an atomic weapon as he started amassing stockpiles of uranium. Heisenberg had published his work on the theory of quantum mechanics in 1925 for which he received the Nobel Prize in Physic in 1932.[1]

Nazi Germany's propaganda ministry assigned the term Wunderwaffe (Wonder Weapon) to their super weapons. They had several that could have caused problems for the Allies if the war had lasted longer.[2]

Aircraft of the Third Reich

The Treaty of Versailles contained the plans for the end of World War I and stated that Germany was forbidden to have any air force. But during the period between the two wars; before the Nazis came to power, German pilots were trained in the Soviet Union.

Established on 26 February 1935, the name given to the Luftwaffe; a generic German term for an air force, sent a detachment of this air arm was sent to fight in the Spanish Civil War, gaining valuable lessons in aircraft and tactics. At the start of World War II, the Luftwaffe became the highest tested in aviation technology and battle experienced any air force in the world.[3]

Germany had several aircraft manufacturers who had experience in the production of aircraft in World War I, who begin to produce aircraft for this new German air force called the Luftwaffe, Some were involved in the creation of Germany's secret weapons.

During the 1930s most military air forces were going from the biplane to the monoplane design. A push was toward a single-engine fighter aircraft but soon some military powers saw that the range of this type of aircraft was limited due to space for fuel. One was the German Ministry of Aviation who issued a request for a new multipurpose fighter called the Kampfzerstorer (Battle Destroyer). It was to be a twin-engine, three-seat, all-metal monoplane with greater range and with a bomb bay.

Several German companies submitted designs that would change the military air force for the coming war in Europe. The following is a description of these types of aircraft and those which led to their designs and their effect on World War II and what might have occurred if the war had continued beyond 1945.

Aircraft manufacturer Dornier Flugzeugwerke in the 1930s designed a light bomber for the Luftwaffe, the Dornier Do 17. It had two engines mounted on a shoulder wing structure with a twin tail fin. It was popular among its crews for ease of handling and harder to hit than other Luftwaffe bombers. The Do 17 first appeared in 1937 during the Spanish Civil War.

It was one of the three main bombers used by the Luftwaffe in the first three years of the war. Production of the Do 17 ended in the middle of 1940 in favor of the Junkers Ju 88 more powerful bomber. 475 were produced in 1939 and 1941.[4]

The Arado Ar 234 Blitz was their most celebrated aircraft of World War II. It was the world's first operational jet-powered bomber. Because of its speed, it was almost impossible to intercept. Its production was limited because it was built during the last days of the war. It was the last German aircraft to fly over England in April 1945.

214 were produced during 1944 and 1945. If the war had continued beyond 1945, this aircraft could have played a major role in the outcome of the war.[5]

The Domier Do 217 first appeared in 1939 as a bomber with a larger bomb load capacity and range than the Do 17. As it developed it was used for dive-bombing and in sea strikes using glide bombs. It was classified as a heavy bomber and served on all fronts and operated as a torpedo bomber, strategic bomber, and reconnaissance aircraft. It performed direct ground assaults and anti-shipping attacks in both the Battle of the Atlantic and the Battle of Normandy. Later in the war, it was converted to a night fighter.

In 1943, the Do 217 was the first aircraft to use the precision-guided Fritz X radio-guided bomb in the Battle of the Mediterranean. It sank the Italian battleship, Roma. 1366 of the Do 217 were produced between 1939 and 1943.[6]

Heinkel Flugzeugwerke AG operating under the restrictions place on German in the Treaty of Versailles prohibiting bombers, designed a mail aircraft for the Deutsche Lufthansa German Airline Company wanting a fast mail carrier for their shorter routes. Heinkel developed the He 70 Blitz (Lightning) in the early 1930s.

The He 70 was a low wing aerodynamically efficient monoplane with retractable landing gear and a nose-mounted single engine of 630 hp using a BMW VI, V-12 ethylene glycol cooled engine instead of water.

To aid in meeting the speed requirements all rivets were flush-mounted producing a smooth surface to minimize drag. This designed allowed the Blitz to set eight-speed records for over distance reaching 234 mph. The pilot and radio operator were seated in tandem with a cabin behind that could seat four passengers facing each other.

The He 70 operated with the airliner from 1934 till 1937 when all of its aircraft were transferred to the Luftwaffe. The Luftwaffe used the Blitz as a light bomber and reconnaissance aircraft. During the Spanish Civil War, twenty-eight aircraft were sent to Spain and used as fast reconnaissance aircraft.

A big drawback for its military use was the He 70 which had a high risk of catching fire. It had a 47-gallon non-sealing fuel tank and part of the airframe was made of extremely flammable magnesium alloy which will burn readily when ignited and is difficult to extinguish. As a military aircraft, the lack of good visibility from the cockpit was a major problem.[7]

The He 70 Blitz was exported to Japan and encouraged the design of the Japanese Val carrier-based light bomber, which saw a lot of action in the war in the Pacific.[8]

Due to the Treaty of Versailles, the early development of German military bombers was disguised as civilian transport aircraft.

Ernst Heinkel, the founder of Heinkel Flugzeugwerke AG was one of the first to try to benefit from Germans' re-armament plan.

In 1933 the Germans did not yet have a State Aviation Ministry but only an aviation commissariat out of the Luftwaffe Administration Office. The head of this administration was hoping to build a new air force out of the German Flying Corps, which dated back before World War I when they were flying balloons. The aviation commissariat knew they needed modern aircraft and visited Ernst Heinkel and convinced him to move his plant from Warnemunde to a factory airfield in the coastal Marienehe region of Rostock.

Heinkel Flugzeugwerke AG was a large company with over 3,000 employees and operated a mass-production plant.

Once moved, Heinkel began to develop a civil airliner, taking his design of the He 70 Blitz further, Heinkel in reality designed a fast medium bomber named the He 111 in 1934.

The He 111 was the most produced bomber for the Luftwaffe in the early part of World War II and continued being produced until September 1944. It was powered by a V12 engine, with a speed of 249 mph and a range of a little over 1200 miles. Between 1939 and 1944, 5656 He 111 were produced.[9]

The He 111H-6 model had a crew of five, pilot, nose gunner, who served as bombardier and navigator, top gunner who served as a radio operator, waist gunner, and turret machine gunner.[10]

Heinkel produced the He 177 to meet the requirement of the German Ministry of Aviation for a long-range bomber to be used in a sustained bombing campaign deep inside Russia. The program started in 1936 under the Bomber A plan. Getting it to the Luftwaffe was delayed due to problems with the engine design. It was designed as a two-engine bomber with the ability to carry a heavy payload, therefore requiring engines with at least 2,000 horsepower. Engines of this design were new and problems occurred, including catching fire in flight.

Once it became operational it had a higher cruising altitude and speed than its Allied counterpart. Most of its use was on the Eastern Front but due to it maturing into a usable design it got to the war too late to play an important role.

If the Japanese had won the Battle of Midway and the war delayed beyond 1945, the He-177 may have affected the course of the war. 1,146 He 177 were produced between 1942 and 1944.[11]

The Junkers Ju 88 was produced by the Junker Aircraft and Motor Works in Dessau, Germany from 1936 to 1945. It was designed as a fast dive bomber that could outrun any Allied fighters of that time. Overcoming problems in its early development, it became the most versatile combat and important aircraft of the war for the Luftwaffe. It was a twin-engine designed as a multirole combat aircraft with three seats and obtained a speed of 360 mph. 9,122 were produced between 1938 and 1944 as the basic design remained unchanged.

Junker also designed and built the Ju 188, a high-performance medium bomber as a follow-up to their Ju 88. The Ju 188 had a larger payload and better performance. It went into production in October 1942. In 1943 it was upgraded with a larger wing area and a pressurized cockpit designed for high altitude work.

It carried a crew of four and had a speed of 310 mph with several variants including the Ju 188J was a heavy fighter, the Ju 188K a bomber, and the Ju 188L a reconnaissance aircraft. Only 466 were built from 1943 till 1944.[12]

The Germans needed aircraft that could reach heights that the Allied bomber was now flying. They considered the Ju 188J, K, and L models because they had a pressurized cockpit that was fully enclosed in the glazed panels of the entire nose of the aircraft. Plus it had the elevator de-icing equipment for long flights at high altitudes. This design was given the name Ju 388.

Deliveries of the Ju 388 started in August 1944 but few Ju 388s were completed before the war ended. It is doubtful if the war continued beyond 1945 if this aircraft would have made any difference in the outcome of the war.[13]

It is recorded that Germany produced 18,499 bombers in World War II. The United States produced over 96,000.[14]

Arado Flugzeugwerke was a German aircraft manufacturer located in Rostock, northeast of Hamburg. Starting in 1924 they began building powered training aircraft, seaplanes, and later bombers.

In 1933, Arado produced the Arado Ar 66 for the Luftwaffe. It was a single-engine, two-seat biplane that became the main pilot trainer for the

Luftwaffe up until the start and into World War II. Arado built some of the first fighter aircraft for World War II, including the Ar 65, a single-engine, single-seat biplane. As Germany was invading Poland, Arado rose to prominence as they produced the Ar 96. A single-engine low wing monoplane, constructed of all metal. It became the standard advanced trainer of the Luftwaffe in World War II.[15]

Arado followed this up with their Ar 196, a reconnaissance shipboard seaplane with a single engine and low wing design. It was to be standard equipment on large German warships. It carried a pilot and observer. It was favored of the pilots as it handled well in the air and on the water.[16]

Blohm & Voss was an old German company in the shipbuilding industry. They built the famous German battleship, Bismarck. Due to financial problems in the 1930s, they expanded into aircraft manufacturing. When the Nazis came to power their business grew with additional shipbuilding including U-boats and aircraft.

As Allied bombers increased over Germany, Blohm & Voss produced the BV 40, a German glider fighter to attack the Allied bombers. It was a small glider with a front-located armored cockpit with the pilot lying in a prone position. It had two cannons but limited ammunition.

Because its time in the air was limited, the glider would fire its weapon at a bomber, glide back to base to be launched again.

Several prototypes were built and the first one was launched in May 1944. Because the war was coming to an end, the project was canceled. If the war had continued beyond 1945, it is doubtful if this weapon would have had any effect on the war effort.[17]

Another aircraft built by Blohm & Voss was the BV 222 called the Wiking. It was a large six-engine German flying boat. It was the largest seaplane to attain production during World War II. It was mainly used for transporting troops.

Blohm & Voss also built the heaviest aircraft ever, the BV 238 flying boat. Powered by six-piston engines and first flew in 1944. Three were under construction when the war ended. If the war had continued longer, the BV 238 would have given Germany an aircraft with a long-range, high payload and speed, perhaps threaten the coast of the United States.[18]

The German Institute for Sailplane Flight designed a high-altitude reconnaissance aircraft fired by rocket power, the DFS 228. The prototype was complete in March 1944 and flew in August. It was a sailplane with long thin wings. The nose was a self-contained pressurized escape capsule for the pilot that could be separated in an emergency. In February 1945 the project was canceled due to the war situation.[19]

The German company Dornier Flugzeugwerke built the Do 335, a heavy fighter using a push-pull engine; one on the nose of the aircraft and the other on the tail. This configuration gave a low aerodynamic drag allowing the aircraft to reach speeds of 474 mph. Its first flight was in October 1943; production started in May 1944 and was the Luftwaffe fastest piston engine of World War II. Unfortunately for the Germans engine deliveries were delayed due to Allied bombing and aircraft was too late for affecting the war. If the war had continued beyond 1945, this weapon could have changed the war outcome.[20]

Designed in the early to mid-1930s and became the backbone of the Luftwaffe was the Messerschmitt Bf 109 along with the Focke-Wulf Fw 190. The Bf 109 first saw service in 1937 during the Spanish Civil War. It was ahead of its time with all-metal construction, retractable landing gear, and an enclosed cockpit and powered by an inverted V12 liquid-cooled engine. It was commonly called the Me 109 by Allied and German crews.

It served as an interceptor, a bomber escort, day and night fighter-bomber, ground-attack aircraft, all-weather fighter, and a reconnaissance aircraft. It was flown by the three leading German aces of World War II, claiming 928 victories. Over 33,000 Me 109 were produced.[21, 22]

Messerschmitt delivered another aircraft to the Luftwaffe, the Bf 110 (unofficially the Me 110). It was a twin-engine heavy fighter and bomber developed in the 1930s. It was a favored of Herman Goring. and was heavily armed with lots of firepower.

The Bf 110 was a heavily armed aircraft and was successful in the early part of the war in Norway, Poland, and France but pilots complained of its lack of maneuverability. In the Battle of Britain, the Bf 110 flew close air support for the German bombers. By July 1942, after the Battle of Britain, the Bf 110 was the first version to be designed specially as a night fighter and saw service as a night fighter attacking Allied bombers of the US 8th Air Force. Most of the German aces of World War II flew the Bf 110 at one time in their careers. 6,170 Nf 110 were produced for the war effort.[23]

In 1942, Messerschmitt improved their Me 210 with a new wing plan, a longer fuselage, and more powerful engines. There were enough changes that the aircraft has renamed the Me 410. It was a heavy German fighter and deliveries started in January 1943 and continued until September 1944, at that point 1,160 Me 410 were produced.

The Me 410 was moderately successful against Allied bombers who were unescorted due to the range of their fighters. When the P-51 Mustangs and the Supermarine Spitfire appeared as escorts for Allied bombers, the Me 410 was no match in a dogfight.

Despite the Me 410 being Hitler's favorite bomber destroyer, it was taken out of service in mid-1944 in favor of the heavily armed single-engine fighters but continued to serve on reconnaissance missions. 1,189 Me 410 were produced.[24]

Gerhard Fieseler Werke in Kassel, Germany was an aircraft manufacturer in the 1930s and 1940s. It produced the Fi 103R, a crew version of the V-1 flying bomb. It was designed to be carried under the wings of a bomber, such as the Heinkel He 111. As the bomber neared the target, the Fi 103R would be released and the pilot would steer the bomb to the target, bailing out at the last moment. It was a suicide mission.

Fieseler produced several variants:

R-I

The basic single-seat unpowered glider. R-II

Unpowered glider; had a second cockpit fitted in a place where the warhead was. R-III

A pulsejet-powered two-seater. R-IV

The standard-powered operational model. R-V

Powered trainer for the Heinkel He 162 (shorter nose).[25]

Manufacturer Anton Flettner, Flugzeugbau GmbH produced helicopters for the Germans in World War II. Their Fl 282, the Hummingbird was a single-seat rotor design. It is recorded as the world's first series-production helicopter.

Its intended role was to ferry items between ships but the German navy wanted to use it for spotting submarines and ordered 15 to be followed by 30 more.

As the war continued, the Luftwaffe's interest increased and they saw a need for its use in artillery and aircraft spotting. They placed orders for what became the B-2 version with a rear seat for an observer in 1945.

The German Air Ministry ordered 1,000 units in 1944 but after 24 were completed the plant was destroyed by Allied bombers. If the war had continued beyond 1945, the Flettner helicopters may have contributed more to the war.[26]

When the German high command began to hear of the B-29 Allied bombers in 1942 and when they started appearing in 1944 flying at altitudes of 26,000 to 33,000 feet well beyond which German's fighters could reach. The German Ministry of Aviation knew that the Luftwaffe needed a high altitude fighter and they turn to Focke-Wulf Flugzeugbau AG in Bremen, Germany, and the well-known Messerschmitt AG in Augsburg, Germany.

Focke-Wulf produced the Ta 152 in three versions; Ta 152H as a high altitude fighter-interceptor, the Ta152C for medium altitude and ground attack operations, and the Ta 152F as a fighter reconnaissance aircraft.

The Luftwaffe received its first Ta152H in January 1945 and was the fastest fighter at 469 mph that the Germans had available. The late entry and the insufficient numbers produced did not affect the outcome of the war. If the war had continued beyond 1945, these high-altitude fighters may have affected.[27] Also to counter the Allied B-29 Superfortresses, Blohm & Voss built their BV 155. It was a high-altitude interceptor aircraft. Work started in 1942 on the design as the Messerschmitt Me155 and merged the design with an in-house study designated it as the Me 409 and later the Bf 109ST. Finally, the new design was designated the Me 155B.[27]

It had a pressured cabin due to high altitude mission and a ceiling of 46,250 feet, late to over 50,000 feet. Prototypes were still being tested as the war ended.

If the war had continued beyond 1945, this aircraft would have been a key weapon against high altitude flying Allied bombers.

In 1937, the German Ministry of Aviation request proposals for a short-range, three-seat reconnaissance aircraft that could support German troops in the field with good intel. Focke-Wulf presented their Fw 189 design with twin engines, twin-boom, and a three-seater.

It first flew in 1938 and entered the Luftwaffe in 1940 and continued being produced unit mid-1944.[28]

Focke-Wulf designed and built the Fw 190 Wurger (Shrike) in the late 1930s. It was a single-seat, single-engine fighter and became the backbone of the Luftwaffe during World War II. It had a twin-row of BMW radial engine.

It became operational with the Luftwaffe in August 1941 with the Fw 190A version. It proved superior to the British Spitfire Mk V in every way except in turn radius. It maintained air superiority until the British introduced the Spitfire Mk IX in early 1943. More than 20,000 Fw 190 were produced making it the second-largest number of aircraft built for the Luftwaffe next to the Messerschmitt Bf 109. [29]

The Reich Air Ministry wanted a lightweight fighter, powered by the BMW 003 axial turbojet engine. They issued a specification for it on 10 September 1944. The specs required that it be designed, built, and fly in the quickest time possible. Plus it had to exceed that of the piston-engine fighters.

Heinkel designed and built the prototype in74 days from the time they received the contract and the first flight. It was named the He 162.

The German Air Ministry thought that this aircraft could be assigned to the Hitler Youth squadron but the plane was so hard to fly if it had ever reached those Youth squadrons many of their pilots would have died just trying to control the aircraft.

One Luftwaffe squadron in February 1945 and another near the Denmark border on 31 March. Due to time the aircraft was never certified ready for combat and had few encounters with Allied aircraft.

Because it was fast at 550mph, if the war had gone beyond 1945, it may have played a more role in the war.[30]

The Heinkel He 219 was a night fighter designed for the Luftwaffe and introduced in the last period of World War II. It was designed with various innovations, including an intercept radar, making it perfect for night missions, with ejection seats; which Heinkel had developed in 1940 for their He 280 prototype jet fighter. It proved it worked when one of Heinkel's test pilots had to use it to save his life in 1942. It was also the first operational military aircraft to have tricycle landing gear.

Due to the late arrival of the engines, the aircraft didn't fly until November 1942. Only 294 models were built by the end of the war and they saw limited service.

This aircraft could have contributed more for the Germans if the war had gone beyond 1945.[31]

Henschel produced the Hs 129, a ground attack aircraft that saw service in Tunisia and on the Eastern Front. As the war continued, the Hs 129 saw success in anti-tank support. It was a twin-engine monoplane with and thick lower mounted wing. Although it was successful as a tank killer, the Luftwaffe did not get enough aircraft to make a difference in the outcome of the war.

If the war continued beyond 1945, Henschel may have time to get more aircraft to the Luftwaffe.[32]

Henschel Hs 132

Henschel was an old German company dating back to the early 18 hundreds. By the 20th century, they had become the largest locomotive manufacturer in Germany. It extended its work into other fields including aircraft.

In 1935 they began manufacturing the Panzer I tanks and became the sole manufacturer of the Tiger tank.

A specification published by the German Air Ministry on 18 February 1943 called for a single-seat attack aircraft to be used in the upcoming Allied invasion of Europe. The design was intended to replace the present-day piston-driven dive bomber due to better performance requirements that a jet aircraft could provide.

Henschel submitted a design in later spring 1944. It had a streamlined, slender, cigar-shaped fuselage with short wings set at the mid-way point. A BMW jet engine was mounted on the back of the aircraft above the wing and behind the cockpit. The cockpit was designed into the fuselage contour with a clear rounded nose-cone at the front of the aircraft allowing for maximum viewing. The pilot flew in a prone horizontal position which had been used before in the Berlin B9 twin-piston experimental aircraft in 1943, showing that the pilot lying down was able to improve his ability to handle high G loads.

A large armored-glass window was located a little distance behind the nose.[33]

The basic A model carried one 1,100 lb. bomb but no other armament. The basic attack method was to enter a shallow dive outside of the ships' range of fire and reaching a speed of 570 mph, the pilot would toss the bomb to the target using computerized sight, then climb back out of range. The aircraft was designed to handle a 12 G pullout. The pilot being in the prone position could handle the G forces better.

Henschel built three different versions, the Hs 132A was their dive bomber design, the Hs 132B was the dive bomber/anti-tank plane and the Hs132C was the dive bomber with a larger engine and higher bomb load.

Due to the lack of many raw materials, the Hs 132 was constructed of many wooden parts. Only one prototype was produced with three others under construction when the Russians overran the plant.

If the war had continued beyond 1945, the Henschel Hs 132 may have become a weapon that the Germans could have used to affect the outcome of the war.[34]

Horton Ho 229 Bomber

Photo by Captain Richard Kik, Jr from Capt. Richard Kik, Jr. Archives/K.S. Kik

In the early 1930s, the Horton Brothers were German aircraft homebuilders and had an interest in flying wing design as a method of improving the performance of gilders. When Hermann Goring, head of the Luftwaffe wanted a new light bomber, the Hortons designed what became known as the Horton Ho 229 bomber. It could fly at 49,000 feet; carry 2,000 pounds of armaments with a range of 620 miles and at speed of 600 MPH. It was powered by twin turbojet engines, with two cannons and two R4M rockets, and was a flying wing design, the first-ever.

It met Goring's approval and the first flight was in March 1944. The Germans tried to build a prototype Ho 229 V3 using sawdust and charcoal over wood to achieve stealth design, the first in the world but the war ended before they could have one flying.[35]

If the invasion of France was delayed the Germans may have had the first stealth long-range, fast, and high flying jet bomber that could have caused the direction of the war to change.

The Germans designed and built three aircraft that could have had a greater impact on the results of the war if it had lasted longer. One was the Me-262 jet fighter, the Me-264 non-jet bomber, and the Ar-234B twin-jet bomber.

Messerschmitt Me-262

Photo from *media.defense.gov/2005/Dec/22/2000574791/-1/-1/0/040820-F-1234P*

The introduction of the North American P-51 Mustang to escort American and British bombers deep into Germany starting in late 1943 brought devastation to Germany with little resistance from the Luftwaffe. Hitler wanted a new fighter that could be mass-produced cheaply, fast, and efficiency. His designers working on the inventions before the war of Britain's Sir Frank Whittle and Germany's Hans-Joachim Pabst von Ohain of the centrifugal and axial flow turbojets developed the first operational jet aircraft.

By the end of 1942, the Messerschmitt Me-262; known as Projekt 1065, was chosen because of its' greater range and speed of over 540 miles per hour. For the first test flight of the Me-262, they installed a piston engine in the nose. It proved more work had to be done because on that first test flight both jet engines failed. Once the engine problems were worked out, the Me-262 went into production.

After halting production in 1943 due to its high fuel consumption, Hitler reinstated production in 1944 with a goal of 1,000 per month.

It was a single-seat aircraft, powered by two Junker 004B-1 jet engines, producing a thrust of 1,980 pounds. It was 100 MPH faster than any allied aircraft at that time. The wingspan was 41 feet with a length of 35 feet and a height of 12 feet, 7 inches high. It weighed 6,396 pounds compared to the weight of the P-51D at a gross of 9,200. The Me262 had a range of 652 miles and an altitude of 37,565 feet. By October 1944 other versions were made for photo-reconnaissance, ground attacks, and a two-seater with radar-equipped for a night fighter model.

The Me262 was armed with four 30 mm MK-108 cannons with a firing rate of 650 rounds per minute. It also carried 24 R4M air-to-air rockets.

On 26 February 1945, Allies sent 1200 bombers to hit Berlin, in that raid the Luftwaffe attacked with 37 Me-262 aircraft, shooting down 16 allied bombers and one allied fighter while losing only three jets.

Throughout the war, it was estimated that the Me-262 shot down 542 Allied aircraft while losing 100 jets.

During the war, 1,433 Me-262s were delivered to the front, mostly used on bombing runs. Its use was limited by a lack of fuel, ammunition, and spare parts. If the war had extended beyond 1945, these limitations may have been overcome.[36]

Arado Ar.234B-2 Blitz

Photo from *aviacionargentina.net*

The world's first operational jet bomber was the German Arado Ar 234 B Blitz built by the German company Arado Flugzeugwerke. It was powered by a Jumo 004 axial-flow turbojet engine with a thrust of 1,80 pounds. The wingspan was just over 46 feet, the height of 14 feet, and the single pilot. The Blitz had a ceiling of 32,810 and a range of 1,103 miles. It was designed for a bomb load of 3,300 pounds. For defense, it carried two 20mm MG 151 cannons firing from its tail. The prototype flew on 15 June 1943. Two production models were built, the B-1 which was a photo-reconnaissance aircraft, and the B-2 was the bomber version. It was the fastest combat aircraft in the world with a speed of up to 540 miles per hour. 214 Ar 234 Blitz called the Lighting were built.

Its first flight was on 15 June 1943 and it appeared on a reconnaissance mission over the beaches of Normandy on 2 August 1944. Only 20 saw action in the Battle of the Bugle in December of 1944 through January of 1945.[37]

Although this aircraft came late in the war and with the United States behind in combat jet aircraft design and manufacturing, if the war had continued beyond 1945, the Ar 234 Blitz could have greatly affected the war effort.

Messerschmitt Me 264 Bomber

Bundesarchiv, Bild 146-1989-039-16A / Fotograf(in): o.Ang.

Hitler wanted a long-range bomber that could deliver weapons to the United States but the technology didn't exist at that time that would allow an aircraft to cross the Atlantic Ocean without refueling.

In the 1930s Messerschmitt; a German aircraft manufacturer named after its design Willy Messerschmitt had a project for a long-range reconnaissance aircraft called the Project P.1061. Taking that design, Messerschmitt developed the Me264 bomber, known as the Amerikabomber for its goal of attacking the United States.

It was designed as an all-metal tube fuselage with a high wing, four propeller engines, tricycle gear, and a heavy multi-paned glass nose. For the long-range mission and to provide comfort to the crew, it featured bunk beds and a small galley with hot plates.

The Me264 was designed to carry a 6.5-ton bomb that would allow Hitler to strike against the United States, perhaps with an atomic bomb. Three were built and the first flew on 23 December 1942. The plan was to fly it from western France to New York City and return.

If the invasion of France had been delayed, Germany may have been able to get this bomber with an atomic bomb on board to the United States.[38]

Messerschmitt Me 163 Komet Rocket

Me 163 191907 on display at the Australian War Memorial.
Photo: Nick-D / CC BY-SA 4.0

The development of the first turbojet engine began in the 1920s while other designers were interested in the potential of preexisting rocket technology. While the turbojet required air to operate, the rocket motors relied on an enclosed propellant that could deliver greater thrust but the drawback was the fast consumption of the fuel.

A German named Alexander Lippisch began working with a glider manufacturer in the late 1930s on a rocket fighter. In 1941 the prototype the Me 162A was produced, it had swept wings for high-speed performance, powered by a liquid-fuel rocket engine. On October 2, 1941, it set a world speed record of 624 miles per hour.

The Me 162A rocket-powered engine burned fuel in just seven minutes of flight, giving a range of only 25 miles. It became known as the Messerschmitt Me163 Komet Rocket-Powered Jet. It was a single-seat, single rocket engine, mid sweepback wing, and semi-tailless. The first thirty were fitted with MG-151 twenty millimeter cannons, later replaced with twin Mk 108 thirty millimeter cannons for more firepower. They were good for short-range targets but lacked long-range accuracy. The Germans put them into mass production, producing 370 before the war ended.

Because they had such a short-range, they were moved to Luftwaffe airfields closer to the targets that the American and British bombers were hitting in repeated attacks.

To make the fighter lighter it wheels was mounted on a trolley for launching allowing the trolley to fall away after takeoff. On landing, it would skip to a stop on its belly.

Testing was complete and the aircraft became operational in 1943 and the first class of 30 pilots reported for training. It was the first and only tailless rocket-powered interceptor to be in operation service. It intercepted its first allied bombers on 16 August 1944 without success. It was later moved to airfields close to where they could protect German synthetic fuel plants. When the Germans could get the Rocket fighters airborne they would use one of two to dive down on allied bombers making one pass as fuel didn't allow a second pass. As their fuel was exhausted they would glide to their airfield and land. Soon the allied fighter would follow them to their airfields before attacking. All total the Germans claimed 16 kills with their Rocket fighter while Allies agreed to only nine. Allies claimed six to nine of the rocket fighters in combat and another nine to accidents.

If the Germans had additional time before the war ended, they had planned to add a double-chambered rocket engine, expanded fuel tanks, and a pressurized cockpit to their Me 163 Rocket Fighter.

Before the war ended the Germans sold their rocket fighter technology to the Japanese, which use that technology to build their version called the J8M Shushui for their navy and the Ki-200 for their air force. They never reached full-scale production for the Japanese before the war ended.

The Komet was the only rocket-powered fighter to enter operational service in World War II. Unsurpassed speeds were its greatest achievement but its high consumption of fuel its downfall.[39]

Zeppelin Rammer

The Germans need more Messerschmitt Me 262 jet fighters to attack the Allied bomber in an attempt to turn the tide of the war. To try and gain control of the air until more Me 262 could be built, the Germans began to use ramming of the Allied bombers. On 4 April 1945 a German pilot flying a Me 262 jet rammed a B-24 after shooting down two B-24 and running out of ammunition.[40]

The Germans established a dedicated squadron called the Sonderkommando Elbe to ram Allied bombers just one month before the end of the war in Europe. Some German pilots did destroy some Allied bombers by ramming, one occurred when a German Bf 109G took out a B-24 named the Palace of Dallas, which was leading a formation of B-24s, the ramming by the Bf 109 destroyed the Palace of Dallas by its wing slicing into the cockpit of the B-24. Although crippled itself the Bf 109 collided with another B-24 while the German pilot bailed out and survived.41[41]

Chapter 10
Secret Weapons of Nazi Germany

Before World War II, Germany had an advantage over many of the countries that they would fight in the coming war in the chemical, steel, and aviation plus in the number and ability of their scientists. This advantage gave the Nazis the power to develop many weapons of war that the world had not before seen. The knowledge and ability of their many scientists would bring rocket technology to the forefront that would change the world during the war and long after.

The world's largest chemical and pharmaceutical company, IG Farben was located in Germany. It was form in 1925 from a merger of six chemical companies, Agfa, BASF, Bayer, Hoechst, Chemische Fabrik Kalle and Cassella. One of IG Farben's subsidiaries supplied the poison gas used in the killing of the Jews in the gas chambers.[1]

IG Farben was involved with the German army's chemical warfare program contributing to the development of nerve agents such as tabun and sarin.[2]

In the 1930s a German company, Vereinigte Stahlwerke AG was the largest steel producer in Europe. It produced about 40% of the steel and 20% of coal and much of the iron for Germany. It would produce steel and power for many of the companies that built weapons for the Third Reich.[3]

Friedrich Krupp AG was the largest company in Europe at the beginning of the 20th century. It was the premier weapons manufacturer in both world wars for Germany. It built U-boats, tanks, battleships, guns, howitzers, and many other items for the Nazis.[4]

Junkers Aircraft and Motor Works (Junkers) was a major producer of German aircraft and aircraft engines. It was a pioneer in all-metal aircraft and built most of the successful Luftwaffe aircraft, including both piston and jet engines.[5]

Heinkel Flugzeugwerke was a German company and a designer of liquid-fueled rockets and turbojet-powered aircraft contributing to high-speed flight before World War II. During the war, they built bomber aircraft for the Luftwaffe.[6]

A German company that produced the most successful fighters for the Luftwaffe in World War II was Messerschmitt AG. Its most famous was the bf 109 and Me 262.[7]

Germany produced many famous scientists that worked during World War II in various fields including some for the Nazis and some without. They included: Max Born - instrumental in the development of quantum mechanics. Arthur Rudolph leader of an effort to develop the V-2 rocket. Kurt Tank designer several important aircraft for the Luftwaffe including the Fw 190 fighter. Walter Dornberger directed the construction of the V-2 rocket and recruited the young Wernher von Braun. Wernher von Braun the most favorite of all German chemical engineers and rocket scientists with his work on the V-2 and later work for NASA in the United States. Johannes Hans Plendl's work as a radar scientist made possible the early bombing successes of the Luftwaffe. Hermann Oberth- one of the founding fathers of rocketry and astronautics.[8]

These were just a few of the many outstanding German scientists that contributed in some way to the future of rockets, aircraft, and missiles for the Third Reich.

Fritz X Bomber

Fritz X Guided Bomb. Photo: Sanjay Acharya / CC BY-SA 4.0

The German Experimental Institute for Aviation was established in 1912 in Berlin and worked on many aircraft designs and weapons for aviation. Starting in the late 1930s work on a controlled bomb was underway.

Finally, in 1943 one made it into production, called the Fritz X Bomber; also known as the Ruhrstahl X-1, the grandfather of smart bombs. It was the first precision-guided weapon to be used in World War II and was designed to be an armor-piercing weapon with a 3450-pound explosive bomb using a radio receiver and highly designed tail controls that could guide the bomb to its target. It was so powerful that it could penetrate 28 inches of armor and could be released from 20,000 feet, well out of the range of anti-aircraft fire. It was carried and launched by a Luftwaffe aircraft but the Luftwaffe aircraft were limited in range and endurance because of the weight of the bomb.

After the fall of Mussolini in Italy on 8 September 1943, the Germans worried that the new Italian government would turn their navy to the Allies. They decided they would attack and sink the Italian Navy before that could happen.

On 9 September 1943 the Luftwaffe flying twin-engine Dornier Do 217 medium bombers, launched from an airfield in Southern France, released two Fritz X bombs against and hitting the newest and largest Italian battleship, the Roma off Sardinia, sinking it in just 35 minutes with heavy loss of lives.[9]

A few days later, the US Navy cruiser, USS Savannah supporting a landing in southern Italy was targeted by a Fritz X. The bomb hit the Savannah at the roof of the number three gun turret, glanced off continuing through the ships handling spaces, passing through the magazine area, exiting the bottom of the cruiser, and exploding as it entered the water. The damage was extensive causing many casualties and serious damage to the ship requiring emergency repairs at Malta then to Philadelphia Naval Shipyard for further repairs.9

On 13 September the German Luftwaffe using the Fritz X attack the British cruiser Garda in the Mediterranean badly damaging it and causing the British to tow it to Malta for repairs.

Finally, the Allies were able to use jamming devices that block the signals to the Fritz. But if the war had continued the Germans would have been able to get around those jamming devices.

If the invasion of France in June 1944 had been delayed, Germany may have been able to get more Fritz X bombs into production and change its design so it couldn't be jammed.

Photo Courtesy of Kirk Steinhoff

In 1941, the German navy mounted a Nebelwerfer (smoke thrower) rocket launcher on the deck of a German submarine. Successful tests were conducted on the surface and from below to a depth of 38 feet. Without a guidance system, it proved to be ineffective.

Success with the V-1 flying bomb, the Germans had a proposal to mount the V-1 and launcher on submarines in 1943 to hit targets up to 150 miles. Because the V-1 was a Luftwaffe weapon and subs were navy, inter-service rivalry killed the project.

Again in 1943 with the success of the V-2 rocket, consideration was given to mount the V-2 and launcher on a submarine that could be used to hit targets in the United States. As the V-2 and launcher were too large for normal German submarines, a 500-ton submersible, none powered, was designed that could be towed within range of the targets in the States by a conventional submarine and the V-2 could be launched. Three such vessels were ordered to be built in late 1944 but only one was completed before the war ended.[10]

If the war had continued beyond 1945, it is possible that such U boat rockets could have been constructed and had an effect on the outcome of the war.

Submarines

The German navy had great success with their submarines and many new designs and changes to old designs were in the works of U Boats as the war was coming to an end. Some changes which could have affected the war effort were:

Type XXI a class of diesel-electric submarines, designed with more batteries allowing it to operate primarily submerged as long as several days and could be recharged via snorkel at periscope depth. Making an improved hull design to the boat increased underwater speed while a design of power assist torpedo reloading allows for faster launching of torpedoes. One hundred and eighteen were rushed into production but only two got to the fleet before the war ended.

Another good German submarine was the type XXVI Walker U Boat-designed with a submerged speed of about 25 knots, 18 knots on the surface, and a diving depth of 1,000 feet. Its design often 21-inch torpedo tubes, all accessed in the forward torpedo room made for better aiming. This design was the first to have its attack center located in the control room.[11]

This class of submarines could have affected the outcome of the war if it had continued beyond 1945.

The surrender of German U-boat 234

Photo by Seaman Harry O'Brien-U.S. National Archives/Record Group 38

Germany built eight of the largest U-boats ever constructed, designated type XB submarine. They were designed for mine laying and sweeping but suffered from a lack of maneuverability and speed. Only two survived the war but one of interest was U-234. While under construction in 1942, U-234 was damaged by Allied bombs. After U-boat U-233 of this class was sunk in 1944, it was decided to change U-234 from a mine-laying submarine to a cargo carrier.

On 25 March 1945, U-234 left Kiel on the Baltic Sea and arrived at Kristiansand, Norway a few days later. She was loaded with special cargo and set sail for Japan. The captain had orders to avoid any possible contact with the enemy. After leaving Kristiansand she ran submerged for two weeks only surfacing for two hours at night.

A shortwave transmission was received on 10 May 1945 announcing Germany had surrendered and instructions were given to proceed to the nearest allied port and surrender. The captain of U-234 decided to head to the United States and surrender.

Onboard U-234 were two Japanese aviation officers, upon hearing of the surrender of Germany, they committed suicide and were buried at sea.

U-234 was boarded by sailors of the destroyer USS Sutton DE 771 at sea on 14 May. They were passed on to a U.S. coast guard cutter and escorted to Portsmouth, New Hampshire Naval shipyard, arriving on 19 May.[12]

Once the crew had been interviewed it was found that the U-boat was bound for Japan with cargo that could help the Japanese in their war effort. The cargo was found to contain mercury, lead, zinc, optical glass, thallium, and tin containers marked "Japanese Army" containing over 1200 pounds of uranium oxide. Also were technical drawings of the Me 262 jet fighter including production plans, forms, and templates. The two Japanese officers who had committed suicide were experts in the Japanese aviation fuel. All these items were packaged and forwarded to Washington. [12]

If the war had been extended because of President Roosevelt's decision to delay the invasion of Europe because of the Japanese victory at Midway and the U-234 got to Japan, the Japanese may have had jet fighters and the atom bomb. The outcome of World War II may have been different.

German Aircraft Carrier

Official U.S. Navy Photo NH 78311 from U.S. Navy Naval History and Heritage Command

The Graf Zeppelin was one of two carriers ordered by the Kriegsmarine (War Navy) Nazis. Construction began on 28 December 1936 and launched on

8 December 1938. It was 861.2 feet long and had a beam of 118.8 with a draft of 27.9 feet. (the US Navy WWII carrier Lexington CV-2 was 888 feet long, beam 107, and draft 32 feet). Graf Zeppelin was designed for 42 aircraft (the Lexington 78).

When World War II started in September 1939 she was 85% complete but she never was fully complete due to other priorities and conflict between the Navy and Luftwaffe and never saw service. A Luftwaffe carrier wing was assigned to the Graf Zeppelin with three squadrons of Messerschmitt Bf-109s and Junkers Ju-87 Stukas. German navy planners saw the need for the carrier tried to convince Hitler to build more carriers but after Hitler replaced the head of the navy planners with a submarine admiral, the carrier project was mothballed. She remained in the Baltic for the duration of the war.[13]

German Tanks

The introduction of the tank in World War I by the British changed war from trench fighting to the entrenchment of modern armored warfare of World War II and brought an end to the horse cavalry.

The German army during the 1920s started to show interest in tanks, called panzers in German. Knowing they were banned in the Treaty of Versailles, they designed what became known as light and large tractors. One of the first was the Leichttraktor, German for light tractor, armed with a 37 mm anti-tank gun. They went on to the Grosstraktor, the large tractor, armed with a 7.5 cm gun. Both of these were built and tested in the late 1920s. In 1934, they built the Neubaufahrzeug, meaning a new construction vehicle. They were built in small numbers and designed to fool the other European powers.

During this process, the Germans developed three different tank designs, the light tank, the medium tank, and the heavy tank.

The Neubaufahrzeug was a heavy tank design and as the German concepts for their use of armor changed, they had little use of these heavy tanks. Only five of this heavy tank were built and only three was any combat and only during the invasion of Norway. Although this tank did not survive or contribute much to the war effort, it did pave the way for other German tanks.

With the Treaty of Versailles hanging over their heads, the German military had to maintain a degree of secrecy in their tank design. Plus the financial crisis of 1929 demanded that any tank design had to be built at a low cost.

In the early 1930s, Germany put out a requirement for a new light tank under five tons. The German firm Krupp Company from Essen was selected to provide the design and produce the new light tank. Testing continued through 1934 and it was named the Landwirtschaftlicher (farm Tractor) because of the limitation on tanks. It was released to the German army in 1936 and eventually called the Panzer I, panzer meaning tank in German.

Hitler coming to power in 1933 and upon seeing what the Panzer I could do, he in 1936 knew this weapon he could use in his fast tactics of the upcoming World War II, which the world had not seen before.

Knowing that infantry was still the soul of an army, Hitler saw that speed in spearhead actions could take an enemy by surprise and conquer them fast. The new German Panzer I was the perfect weapon for his offense. It saw notable action in the early times of the war, rolling through Poland and France and creating the term Blitzkrieg.

Although many changes were made to the Panzer I, mainly in its armament, engines, and increase in weight, but by 1944, almost all of the Panzer Is had been destroyed in combat.

Slowly the Panzer I was replaced by the Panzer II which had been in development since 1936. The Panzer II production began in 1937.

Having suffered greatly in World War I, France began to construct in the 1930s and completed in 1935, what became known as the French Maginot Line. It was a network of concrete bunkers, a man by machine gun nest, vehicle traps, artillery houses, and steel obstacles that ran along the French border with Germany.

It was thought that any attack along this border will take long enough for France to prepare to defend itself.

Hitler knew this line existed decided that the German army needed a weapon that could breach this line. It had to tie into his new mechanized doctrine.

The Germans knew that to defeat these strategic points of the French Maginot Line would require a special vehicle, one that could keep pace with the new mechanized doctrine of the German Army and one with armament capable of defeating the thick concrete houses of the Maginot Line. Work on such a vehicle began in 1938 under the Krupp banner and evolved considerably along the way.

Starting in 1935 Daimler-Benz began the production of a medium tank to be called the Panzer III and was to be capable of attacking and destroying opposing tank forces. The first Panzer III came off the production line in 1937 and was the main tank of the German Panzer divisions during World War II. It continued to be produced up till 1943 with over 5700 built.

The German company Krupp-Grusonwerk help design and built the first Panzer IV, designed for infantry support. It was intended to work along with the Panzer III, offering support for the infantry and anti-tank support.

The final version had a Maybach HL 120 TRM 12 cylinder gasoline engine with 296 hp and a crew of five, consisting of commander, gunner, loader driver, and radio operator who also serviced as a bow machine gunner.

After it came online in 1939, somewhere between 8,800 and 9,800 Panzer IV tanks were built before the war ended. She became the workhorse for the German army.[14]

As time passed the roles between the Panzer III and Panzer IV switched each assumed the other role.

Tiger

Bundesarchiv - CC BY-SA 3.0 - Tiger

During World War II Germany built four types of tanks. Three in a heavy class; which included the famous Tiger Tanks, seven in a medium class, which included the Panzer series III, IV, and V, and six in a light class, which included the Panzer series I and II. The fourth class was the Reconnaissance series tanks; which had two types. One was a Heavy Reconnaissance tank of which they built 22 and one was a Tracked Reconnaissance Vehicle of which 70 were built. The Tracked Vehicle was a fast go-ahead vehicle that would locate and radio back the enemy location. They replaced the cavalry units of the past.[15]

Panzer

Bundesarchiv Bild 1011-721-0398-21A - Panzer

Hitler had a concern over combating the British tanks and antitank guns. The British had been using their 2-pound anti-tank gun when the war started but by April 1942 in North Africa, they introduced their 6-pounder, 57 MM gun. The ammunition was a basic armor-piercing shot that could destroy the standard German tank.

Britain went through several tank designs during the war with little success and finally switched to the American Sherman tank.

Hitler was concerned about the British anti-tank guns but when he invaded Russia on 22 June 1941 and encountered the Russian T-34 medium tank and the Kv-1 heavy tank. Both were superior to what the Germans had in the field. Hitler demanded the design and production of a new heavy tank to replace the lighter ones in the field.

Two German companies competed in the design, Porsche and Henschel. Henschel won and began production of what would become the Tiger I tank. It had a crew of five, commander, gunner, loader, driver, and radio operator. It had a deadweight of over 55 tons, thicker armor, a larger main gun, more fuel storage, a larger engine, better-built transmission, and suspension with greater ammunition storage. It had an over road speed of 28 MPH and off-road at 13 MPH with a range of 120 miles. Production began in August 1942 at 25 per month increasing to 104 by April 1944. It took twice as long to build a Tiger I than any other German tank. Between April 1942 and August 1944, 1,350 Tiger I was delivered to the front. It was phased out in 1944 as the Tiger II came into production.

In combat, the Tiger tank had its original goal of forming into strike groups of 20 tanks as a spearhead for the lighter panzer division's tanks. During the war, it saw action in Italy, Sicily, Tunisia, Russia, and northwest Europe.

The heavyweight of the Tiger I at 56 tons was beyond the 35-ton weight of the small bridges in Europe so the Tiger I was designed to ford waters up to 15 feet deep using a snorkel and other equipment which allowed it to operate in the water.

The Tiger tank cost over twice what a Panzer IV did but was very successful having destroyed over 10,300 enemy tanks. Its 88 mm gun was capable of penetrating the differential case of the American M4 Sherman tank from 1.3 miles and the turret front at 1.1 miles. But the Tiger gun was not able to penetrate the upper sloped front plate at any range. The American Sherman M4 couldn't penetrate the Tiger frontally at any range.

The appearance of a Tiger in an engagement brought fear to all Allied soldiers and equipment operators.

The Tiger I tank was so successful for the Germans that Henschel was asked to design a bigger tank. They designed and built what became known as the Tiger II or referred to as King Tiger. Using almost the same parts as the Tiger I but weighing in at 70 tons in full combat configuration. Additional armor protection accounted for most of the weight. It was a great weapon and if the war had not ended as it did, this tank along with other super weapons the Germans were developing, the war could have had a different ending in Europe.[16]

Panther Tank

The Panther tank had been considered by some as the best tank in World War II.

It had problems that limited its effect on the battlefield. It was subject to fires because the fuel pumps, carburetors, and fuel lines were prone to leakage which led to gasoline pooling in the engine compartment. Driving up a slope could cause this to slosh onto hot engine parts and catch fire. Many Panthers sent to the Eastern Front were reported unfit for combat due to mechanical problems. It suffered from high fuel consumption and engine overheating. As later models were heavier, the drive train and engine had not been designed to handle the extra weight.

If the war had continued changes to the Panther tanks would have made it better by correcting all of these problems which limited its operation with its current design.

Due to the pressure, the Allied bombing was doing to the Germans, many weapons they were designing and producing only saw limited action or any at all. If the Japanese had won at the Battle of Midway and the invasion of Europe in 1944 had been delayed, some of these weapons may have been a factor in the war.

Some of these were:

The Flakpanzer IV Kugelblitz (Ball Lighting)- The German Air Force from 1943 on was less and less able to protect its forces from Allied bombers which led to the German Armed Forces calling for a special self-propelled anti-aircraft gun. A sketch from a German first Lieutenant was given to a German general who approved his sketch for this new anti-aircraft weapon and Daimler-Benz was chosen to design and built the Kugelblitz.

What made the Kugelblitz different from other self-propelled anti-aircraft guns it was fully enclosed with a rotating turret. In its first proposal, the Kugelblitz was to be mounted on U-boats using the Panzer IV chassis. This idea proved to be impractical and was canceled.

The Kugelblitz was then designed as an anti-aircraft gun using the chassis and the basic superstructure of the Panzer IV tank. Five prototypes were built and mass production was planned but never occurred due to Allied bombing.

Krupp company designed what became known as the Panzerkampfwagen VIII Maus (Mouse) in late 1944. It was a German super-heavy tank, over 33 feet in length, 12 feet 2 inches wide, and 11.9 feet high. It was the heaviest fully enclosed armored fighting vehicle ever built. Its 128 mm gun was powerful enough to destroy any Allied armored vehicle in service.

The Maus weight 188 metric tons and too heavy to cross many bridges and was designed with a snorkel to ford many rivers up to 26 feet. The intend of the Maus was to punch holes through enemy defenses without taking any damage to its components.

Five were ordered but on two hulls and one turret was complete before the Russian overran their production plant.[17]

A strange weapon that the Germans built during World War II was the Kugelpanzer (spherical Tank). It was a one-man vehicle for light reconnaissance, powered by a single-cylinder two-stroke engine. It was spherical and it appears that only one was built and it was shipped to Japan. It was captured by the Russians in 1945 most likely in Manchuria and now on display in Moscow's Kubinka Tank Museum. It is not known if it was ever used in combat.[18]

Toward the end of the war, the Germans built the Panzerkampfwagen E-100, it was a super-heavy tank and the largest tank of the German E-Series. The E-Series was based on a standardized series of tank designs broken into five different weight classes, E-10, E-25, E-50, E-75, and the heaviest the E-100.

Moving into the final year of the war, the Germans want a simpler, cheaper, and more efficient tank than what they had been building in the past. A single E-100 prototype with 150 mm and a 75 mm gun was being built as the war ended.

If the war had continued beyond 1945, the E-Series of German tanks may have greatly affected their war effort.[19]

German Anti-Tank Weapons

The invasion of the Soviet Union in Operation Barbarossa on 22 June 1941 hadn't been as quick as Hitler planned. It had grown into a stalemate until the German army encounter the Soviet T-34 medium tank. After meeting it in combat in 1941, a German general said it was the finest tank in the world. Its three-inch tank gun had no equal and its 60 degrees sloped armor was excellent against anti-tank weapons. Hitler knew that he had to have a weapon capable of destroying these heavier armored tanks.

To answer this call, the German developed a more practical weapon, the tracked, self-propelled tank destroyer which would have penetrating armor power while having the advantage of mobility. An early one in this field was the Sturer Emil, German for Stubborn Emil. It was designed in 1941 as a self-propelled anti-tank gun and only two were produced, both in 1942. It had a 5-inch gun that could move seven degrees to each side, elevate ten degrees and depress 15 degrees, and carried 15 rounds.

The two that were built went to the Eastern Front, one was destroyed and the other captured at Stalingrad in January 1943.[20]

With the Soviet T-34 tank still giving the Germans problems, the German company Alkett (Altmarkische Kettenwerke GmbH) in February 1942 designed a tank destroyer using pats from the Panzer III and Panzer IV tanks. It used a long barrel 8.8 cm anti-tank gun and took the main armament of the Tiger II tank and mounted it on the rear of the chassis. Due to the long barrel of the gun, the length of the hull had to lengthen including moving the engine to the rear. The crew was protected from small arms fire but won't hold up to armor-piercing rounds. This design was not intended for the tank destroyer to engage in tank fights but to provide fast movement of an anti-tank gun.

The German company Krupp at their weapons factory begin developing an 88 mm anti-aircraft gun in 1933 called the Flak 18. Because of its high performance of up to twelve strokes per minute, Krupp designed an anti-tank version named the "88". The drawback was the difficulty of transporting it. Krupp added a shield that rests on two steel wheels making it easier to transport, which became known as the Pak 43.

It was called the Nashorn (Rhino in English) and was mounted on a specially designed Geschutzwagen (armored car) III/IV tank chassis. They used the driving and steering system of the Panzer II and the suspension and engine of the Panzer IV.

With Hitler's approval, this tank destroyer entered into production in early 1943, and 494 were produced mostly in 1943.

The Nashorn first saw action in the Battle of Kursk on the Eastern Front against the Russian in 1943 and performed well. Because of its long firing range, it was able to engage the enemy from a distance, leaving it beyond the firing distance of Russian tanks. Long-range firing from a Nashorn in May 1944 disabled a Russian S-1 tank at a distance of 2900 feet. In March 1945, a US Army M26 Pershing heavy tank was disabled at under 300 yards by a Nashorn near Cologne. [21]

It was the largest and most powerful anti-tank gun to see continuous service with the German army and one of the best anti-tank guns of any kind in World War II. Its maximum velocity was a little over 3600 ft/sec and could penetrate the front armor of any Allied tank including the Soviet T-34 at about 3800 yards with a tungsten shot. Luckily for most US tanks most of the PAK 43 saw action on the Eastern Front early in the war.[22]

Pak 43 On a Tiger III/IV

In January 1944 Hitler approved a newer fully-casemented tank destroyer named the Jagdpanzer IV. It had a lower silhouette with thicker frontal armor and a 7.5 cm gun. This weapon continued in production till 1945.

The United States introduced the Super Pershing in the last weeks of 1945 to combat the German King Tiger. In April 1945 it was reported that a US Super Pershing went head to head with the German King Tiger in Dessau; this event has been questioned by historians if it was a King Tiger or just a Tiger or a Panzer IV.

The action in Dessau is described by the Super Pershing crew as the crew was expecting to encounter German troops but was surprised to see a German tank as they rounded a corner. The German tank fired first but the shot was high. The Super Pershing fired but bounced off the German tank, The German tank rolled forward and climb over some obstacles in the street, exposing its belly. The Super Pershing fires into the belly of the German tank destroying it.[23]

V-3 Cannon

Photo from *historylearningsite.co.uk* 21 Apr 2015

The V-3 was the unnecessary younger sibling of the V-1 and V-2 rockets that pulverized London during the Blitzkrieg. Coming online to the summer of 1944 and called the High-Pressure Pump or often the London Gun, and given the nickname Busy Lizzie.

The V-3 was the largest gun ever manufactured and had a 416-foot barrel with a six-foot bore that operated with a series of charges. The primary firing charge forced the projectile up the long barrel followed by a series of secondary charges located in chambers along the length of the barrel at three yards apart. These would fire electronically, adding pressure and increasing the speed of the projectile. These projectiles were nine feet long, finned and had a 300-pound high explosive warhead, and could fire the dart-shaped shells at a rate of 300 shells per hour. Due to their size, the Busy Lizzies had to be built on a hillside to support its massive weight. They were placed in concrete-lined tunnels on hills in the area of Pas-de-Calais in northern France.

The design called for it to be a high-speed weapon, allowing the shell to get to London from France in an hour, once in operation, the speed was less by about half. It had a range of about 102 miles. Additional work had to be done to increase the speed but the ending of the war canceled that re-design. [24]

This weapon had great potential of the war had continued beyond 1945.

Schwere Gustav Heavy Cannon Railway Gun

Photo from Josep Marimon Collection

In the 1930s the French began fortifications that would protect their territories from an invasion as they had experienced in World War I. These fortifications were called the Maginot line. French newspapers published details of these fortifications which attract the attention of the German armed forces. After studying these details the German military realized they did not have a weapon that could penetrate those fortifications.

Hitler in 1936 asked the Krupp armament to design and build such a weapon. They designed what became known as the Schwerer Gustav 33.5 inches (80cm), weighing 1,350 tons, and could fire a 7-ton shell 29 miles.

This heavy cannon gun was an 800mm (31.5") artillery piece mounted on a railroad car. It was given the security code name Dora. Hitler approved the production in 1939. Two were built but none ready at the battle for France. The gun used two types of shells, an armor-piercing type weighting 7.1 tons and could pierce 3.3 feet of rolled steel armor or 22.9 feet of reinforced concrete. The other type of shell was a high explosive type, weighing 4.8 tons, and would leave a 30-foot crater.

This weapon was huge as the complete barrel 106 feet 7 inches long with its' rifling .39 inches deep. It was mounted to a cradle that held four hydraulic recoil absorbers. The gun used a diesel-powered generator to run the system. It took 25 railroad cars to transport the gun. Allied bombing of the factories producing this weapon ended their use as the war ended.[25]

The gun was designed to be mobile and required four parallel rail tracks traveling on four trains, complete with anti-aircraft gun cars. A crew of 5,000 men was required for the anti-aircraft crews, guards, and operators of the gun.

The Dora was tested fired on 25 November 1941. It was first brought into use in January 1942 against the city of Sevastopol in Russia, firing 47 rounds into the city wearing out the barrel. Eight shells were fired again into Sevastopol on 5 June 1942. Her last action was on 25 June 1942 with five shells into Sevastopol then after moving to Leningrad she was moved back to Germany after the Russian counter-attack and remained there through the rest of the war.

If the war had continued beyond 1945; due to the size of the rounds and its firing distance, this large weapon may have affected the war.

Krupp 5 Rail Gun

Photo by Firearms Central 28cm Kanone 5

In addition to building the huge Schwere Gustav Heavy Cannon Railway Gun, the Krupp Company built 25 smaller railway guns for the Germans called the Krupp 5 or commonly referred to as the K5. It was a heavy railway gun with a massive 71 ft long barrel. Due to its limited traverse, it required a curved stretch of tracks from a cross-track or what is known as the "Vögele Turntable". Using the turntable when available allowed the weapon to have the capacity to turn 360 degrees.

It fired a huge 11.1-inch shell, containing 67 or 98 pounds of TNT weighing 550 pounds up to 40 miles.

The K5 was used against the Allies in their amphibious landings at Anzio, Italy where it helps bring the invasion to a standstill for almost three months. Eight K5s were placed in France with three of those along the English Channel.[26]

Karl-Geret (Karl Device)

The Karl-Geret was a self-propelled gun, manufactured by the German company Rheinmetall at its plant in Dusseldorf using forced labor. Know by their nicknames Thor, Odin, and Loki.

These guns were made from 1940 till 1944. It was powered by a Daimler-Benz 12 cylinder engine for petrol and another for diesel. It was heavy at 124 tons which created a logistical problem. To be moved any distance it had to be dissembled into seven loads using a special mobile crane. When it came to a bridge not strong enough for the weight, it had to be unloaded and each piece carried across separately. For long-distance, it was carried by rail, for shorter routes it moved under its power at a top speed of 6.2 mph.

It had an extra-long barrel of 37 ft and a diameter of more than 10 ft in width. It could fire a two-ton projectile over six miles. Seven were produced and six saw action against the Allies. Most were used against the Soviets on the Eastern Front and four were moved in September 1944 against Warsaw.[27]

The Germans brought the Karl-Gerat super heavy gun to the Ludendorff Bridge over the Rhine which the US forces had captured on 7 March 1945. Both the Americans and Germans employed new weapons and tactics to take or destroy the bridge into Germany. In addition to the Karl-Gerat gun, they fired mortars, howitzers, used floating mines, and air attacks with their Arado Ar 234B-2 turbojet bombers.

The American forces moved in the largest concentration of anti-aircraft weapons used in World War II. This was the last action of the Karl-Gerat gun against Allied forces at Remagen Bridgehead where the German High Command war diary entry reports 14 rounds were fired on 20 March 1945.[28]

If the war had continued beyond 1945, more of this great gun would have most likely have been built and could have affected the war.

Atomic Bomb and Rockets

The Atomic Bomb and the Rockets of the Third Reich were the two programs that the Germans were developing that showed the greatest threat to the Allies. The V-1 and V-2 rockets were used against Great Britain and the development of advanced rockets as the A9/10 planned for attacks on the United States had greater potential.

A complete chapter has been devoted to these two weapons:

Other Projects

As the Third Reich came to power, they were concerned about their reliance on food imported from aboard. They approached Germany's and the world's biggest chemical company I.G. Farben to develop a new insecticide to prevent pests from destroying the food supply. A young chemist named Gerhard Schrader started the work on 23 December 1936 and he built a compound he called Preparation 9/91. It was a high poison causing vomiting, pupil dilation, sweating, diarrhea, shortness of breath, and death in some animals. IG Farben becoming aware of its toxicity to humans alerted the German military about this new poison compound.

When German army scientists at the Spandau Citadel; which serviced as a secret chemical warfare center, first analyzed Schrader's Preparation 9/91, they were so impressed by its toxicity that they named it tabun, after the German word for taboo, tabu. Existing chemical weapons such as mustard gas and phosgene took hours to days to kill victims, but tabun required only 20 minutes. It was a clear, colorless, and tasteless liquid having a fruity faint odor. It was an extremely toxic chemical that affects the normal function of the nervous system and is usually fatal. It was the first of a series of nerve agents.[29]

As WWII was on the horizon, the German military built a tabun pilot plant capable of producing 400 kg of the poison at a site called Raubkammer near the city of Münster in the western part of Germany. They tested aerial bombs containing tabun and discovered that the most deadly way to deploy the not-so-volatile agent was to use a small detonation to disperse it as a mist.

By the spring of 1943, a few years into the war, the first large-scale tabun factory near Dyhernfurth, a small town 40 km away from what is now Wrocław, Poland, was producing 350 metric tons (350,000 kg) of tabun per month. By the end of the war, the factory had produced 12,000 metric tons of tabun and loaded it into aerial bombs and artillery shells.

German military researchers began to weaponize tabun, looking for means of putting its safety into projectiles without spillage. They tested it on animals and tried to find an antidote.

At the long battle of Stalingrad which started in August 1942, the Germans were advancing as the Russians were being pushed back until the Russians launched a two-pronged attack in November which pushed the German army back. In May 1943, the German leadership urged Hitler to use tabun and other chemical weapons to push the Russians back but Hitler objected and ordered no chemical weapons be sent to the Russian front.

Records show that at a meeting in the Wolf's Lair in May 1943, Hitler was told by German chemists Otto Ambros, who had become the head of the plant where tabun gas had been developed, that Germany had 45,000 tons of chemical gases stockpiled but that the Allies may have more. Fearing retaliation from the Allies may have been the reason Hitler objected to their use, plus he had personally experienced gas in World War I.

"He thought there would be retaliation—if not in kind," said David H. Moore, a toxicologist and former official at the United States Army Medical Research Institute of Chemical Defense, at the Aberdeen, Proving Ground in Maryland. "That's the common explanation."

In 1938, another German scientist created a nerve agent twice as toxic as tabun and applied it to monkeys. He brought it to the fortress Spandau Citadel in Berlin, which had been set up as a secret chemical weapon development center. Their chemists began to study its effects and develop means of producing it. Taking letters from the last names of the scientists who had last worked on this agent, Schrader, Otto Ambros, Gerhard Ritter, and Hans-Jürgen von der Linde, they named it Sarin. This new agent was more volatile and toxic than tabun but harder to manufacture. It soon became clear to the German military that sarin was a better gas than Taban and in1943, Germany approved the construction of a new factory about 70 miles outside Berlin to manufacture sarin.[30]

The Allies had no idea that the German military had discovered and was stockpiling a suite of extraordinarily toxic chemical weapons. But they could, and should, have known. In May 1943, after Germany lost a six-month battle in Tunisia, Allied forces took some 230,000 Axis soldiers prisoners. Among these prisoners of war was a German who informed British interrogators that he was a chemist who had worked at a secret chemical weapons institute—the Spandau Citadel in Berlin—on a new poison with "astounding properties." His descriptions of the colorless, nearly odorless chemical that could kill victims in just 20 minutes sounded like it might be too good to be true. Although the soldier's interrogators believed the story, British intelligence officers back in England did not. The 10-page report filed by the interrogators was ignored.[30]

At the interrogation of Herman Gorman, he was asked why the Germans didn't use chemical weapons at Normandy. He replied that the army relied on horse-drawn transportation to move supplies to their combat units and they didn't have any mask that would fit horses.[31]

In the summer of 1942, the head of the University of Chicago's Metallurgical Laboratory, Arthur Compton wrote that the United States needed to protect against ionizing bombs. It was thought that the Germans would have within the next few months enough radio-active materials to make bombs that could spread radiation over drop areas. It was suggested that the United States government should develop means of detecting.

A detection device was manufactured to detect high levels of radiation and secretly placed in Manhattan District offices in New York, Chicago, Boston, San Francisco, and Washington, DC.

If the Germans did use radiological weapons, it was to be used as an area-denial weapon, making an area uninhabitable for a time, or to contaminate critical areas such as airports, or to attack troops, or against large cites to create panic.[32]

In March 1944, General Eisenhower became aware of the possibility that the Germans might use such a weapon against the invasion force of Europe and created Operation Peppermint. This operation was to deploy radiation monitoring during the D-Day invasion. Dry runs were conducted on German bomb craters and no evidence of radiological weapons was detected and Operation Peppermint was never placed into action.[33]

Synthetic Fuel

Germany had an abundant coal reserve but little to no petroleum deposits. Before the twentieth century, this was not a problem, homes and commercial businesses used coal for heating. Many of the machinery in their industrial plants also used coal. Most commercial and military ships used coal at this time. But with the invention of the combustion engine, the creation of the automobile, the airplane, and the increased use of trucks made gasoline and diesel fuel a must.

Not long after 1900; knowing that new fuels would be needed to meet the demands of the German economy for the combustion engine. Friedrich Bergius, a German chemist working for the German chemical giant, I.G. Farben in 1913 developed a process that became known and the Bergius Process. His process put high-volatile bituminous coal under high pressure and temperature to create a liquid hydrocarbon therefore a synthetic fuel, a liquid that could be used to power the combustion engine. This process was known as the direct conversion method.

After World War I in 1919 this process was put into production at a plant operated by Goldschmidt AG in Berlin.[34]

In 1923 two Germans, Franz Fischer and Hans Tropsch developed a process of indirect conversion of coal by the gasification of coal and converting it into synthetic fuel.[35]

I.G. Farben, the German chemical giant who in 1925 was formed when six chemical companies, BASF, Bayer, Chemische Fabrik Griesheim-Elektron, Hoechst, Agfa and Weiler Ter Meer to be the world leader in chemistry, patented Bergius process in 1926. The company argued that synthetic fuels from coal could cut Germany's dependence on foreign oil and also reduce the pressures on foreign exchange.

Upon meeting with Farben officials in 1933, Hitler endorsed the idea of making synthetic fuel from coal. He knew that fuel had to be available for what he wanted to accomplish for his Third Reich.

The talk had become earlier on a system of highways across Germany but nothing had occurred until Hitler came to power. In September 1933 he ceremonial shoved dirt to start the first autobahn at Frankfurt. He also had plans for a cheap car for the German people. In 1937 his government formed a state-owned company to produce such a car. That company became known as Volkswagen. His quest for German power would require tanks, trucks, bombers, and fighter planes all requiring fuel and oil. Synthetic fuel produced by I.G. Farben would become vital to Hitler's goals. By 1938, I.G. Farben had been Nazify and all Jews with the company had been removed.

In 1935, the Hibernia Mining Company founded the first coal liquefaction plant at Gelsenkirchen Germany, and began operation in 1936, achieving a capacity of 200,000 tons/year of mainly aviation base gasoline. After 1937, a Nordstern plant was opened for converting bituminous coal to synthetic oil.35

By August 1939, Germany had twelve operational hydrogenation plants producing gasoline and mineral oils, with a total capacity of 3.85 million tons a year. These covered most of the Wehrmacht's needs for fuel and lubricants in case of war.

Allies leaders had targeted German oil industries as early as 1940 but they were focusing on German cities and other industries such as aircraft manufacturers. Due to heavy losses of Allied bombers from anti-aircraft fire and Luftwaffe aircraft, the 8th Air Force out of England and the 15th out of Africa had to wait until the P-51 aircraft was in the fight to join their bombers on the way to their targets in Germany.

When Allied bombing of the German synfuels plants began taking its toll in late 1944 and early 1945, the entire Nazi war machine began grinding to a halt. More than 92 percent of Germany's aviation gasoline and half its total petroleum during World War II had come from synthetic fuel plants. At its peak in early 1944, the German synfuels effort produced more than 124,000 barrels per day from 25 plants. In February 1945, one month after Allied forces turned back Hitler's troops at the Battle of the Bulge, German production of synthetic aviation gasoline amounted to just a thousand tons one-half of one percent of the level of the first four months of 1944. None was to be produced afterward. Lack of petrol meant the end of the war and the end of the Third Reich. If the war had continued beyond 1945, Germany synthetic fuel production could have increased its volume to an overall high, continuing fueling the Nazi machine.

Chapter 11
Other Weapons

Some secret weapons were conceived but never happened; others made it off the drawing board but never contributed to the war effort.

The Landkreuzer P 1500 Monster

Photo by *history.net* - Illustration by Jim Laurier

In June 1942, the German Ministry of Armament proposed a 1,000-ton tank. Friedrich Krupp AG; a premier weapon manufacturer for Germany in both world wars, was given the contract.

In December Hitler gave the go-ahead for the project and the design was increased from 1,000 tons to 1,500 tons. It was the heaviest artillery weapon ever constructed when you look at total gun and shell weight. It was designed to fire a 7-ton projectile up to 23 miles.

The Monster was 138 feet long and would have weighed 1500 tons. Its armor would have been 250 millimeters thick and propelled by four submarine diesel engines. It would have needed a crew of over one hundred to operate.

Its principal armament was to be an 800 mm Schwerer Gustav K (E) railway gun. This would have been mounted on a fixed turret so that the Landkreuzer would have been a self-propelled gun rather than a tank.

Such a gun would have been able to launch shells without having to directly engage the enemy. Two 150 mm SFH 18/1 L/30 Howitzers and several 15mm MG 151/15 autocannons would have added to its power.

Albert Speer, Minister for Armaments in 1943 canceled the project due to other more needed armaments for the war effort. If the war had continued beyond 1945, this weapon may have gone back into production and become a factor in the outcome of the war.

No prototypes of the Landkreuzer were made.[1]

Battleships

The Germans built a pair of fast battleships; known as the Bismarck class, just before World War II. Both were the largest and most powerful ships built for the German Nazi Navy. Weighing over 41,000 metric tons with a top speed of 30 knots and carrying eight 15 inch guns. The Bismarck was laid down in July 1936 and completed in September 1949. Her sister ship, the Tirpitz was laid down in October 1936 and completed in February 1941.

The Bismarck conducted only one mission, Operation Rheinubung which was a raid into the North Atlantic to attack convoys from American to England. During this raid, she attacks and sunk the British battlecruiser HMS Hood and damaged the new British battleship Prince of Wales. The British launched a major operation to find and sink the Bismarck. After a three-day chase, she was sunk.

Her sister ship, the Tirpitz operated in the Baltic Sea in 1941 and was sent to the Norwegian waters in 1942. Her mission was to attack the British convoys supplying the Soviet Union. Finally, British Lancaster bombers on 12 November 1944 dropped three of the five-ton Tallboy bombs causing a magazine explosion that capsized the ship.

Hitler in early 1939 order a plan to re-equip and expand the German Navy, the Kriegsmarine. This plan was given the name Plan Z and was the challenge of the most powerful navy in the world, the British Navy. This plan had been in the strategic thinking of the German Naval High Command since the end of World War I.

The plan called for ten battleships, four aircraft carriers, numerous long-range cruisers, and a small force of U-bouts. The first phase of this plan was designed H-39, which called for six ships to be built. The Oberkommando der Marine (OKM), the High Command of the Navy; who was the highest administrative and command of the Kriegsmarine, issued requirements for a ship of 35,000 long tons with eight 15 inch guns and a speed of 30 knots.[2]

Several designs followed with the H-41 for larger 16.5-inch guns and reinforced deck armor. The H-42 and H-43 with 18.9-inch guns and increased the main battery. The H-44 followed with 20-inch guns and displacement of over 55 thousand long tons. All designed with a speed of more than 30 knots.[3]

Germany had only four shipyards large enough to build the six new battleships. The OKM issued orders to construct the first two ships on 14 April 1939. The contract for the other four was on 25 May 1939. The keels for the first two ships were done at Blohm & Voss dockyard in Hamburg and at the Deschimag shipyard in Bremen in July and September 1939.

When war broke out in September 1939 work on the first two was suspended and the laying of the keel for the other four was canceled.[4, 5]

Japanese Victory at Midway may have allowed these battleships to have entered the war, challenging both the British and American navies. The results of World War II may have been different.

The Junker Ju 322 Mammut

Photo from a model by Anigrand Craftworks

In 1940, work was started on a heavy military glider that could be used to transport a large number of troops or heavy equipment such as a tank. Junkers Aircraft and Motor Works, who in World War I had pioneered all-metal aircraft, started the design and construction.

When the Nazis came to power in 1933, they demand that the founder of the company, Hugh Junker, turn over all of his company patents to the Nazis. When he refused he was arrested, jailed and the Nazis took over his company.

This design looked like a large flying wing with stabilizing fins and a rudder made entirely of wood due to the war effort and lack of metal. The cockpit was to the port side above the cargo bay and armed with three MG15 machine guns.

It was named the Junker Ju 322 Mammut and was proposed to be used by the Luftwaffe to carry troops or heavy equipment such as a tank with weight up to 44,000 pounds. For takeoff, it used a large trolley with eight pairs of wheels and it landed with four separate sprung landing skids.

Two prototypes were built and the first test flight was in April 1941, which proved to be a disaster. Several other flights were made but the project was canceled in May 1941. The other prototype never flew and was finally destroyed. Although the original plans called for 100 aircraft and 30 were in production when the project was canceled. It proved to not be an effective weapon and would have not affected the outcome of the war if it had continued beyond 1945.[6]

The Sun Gun

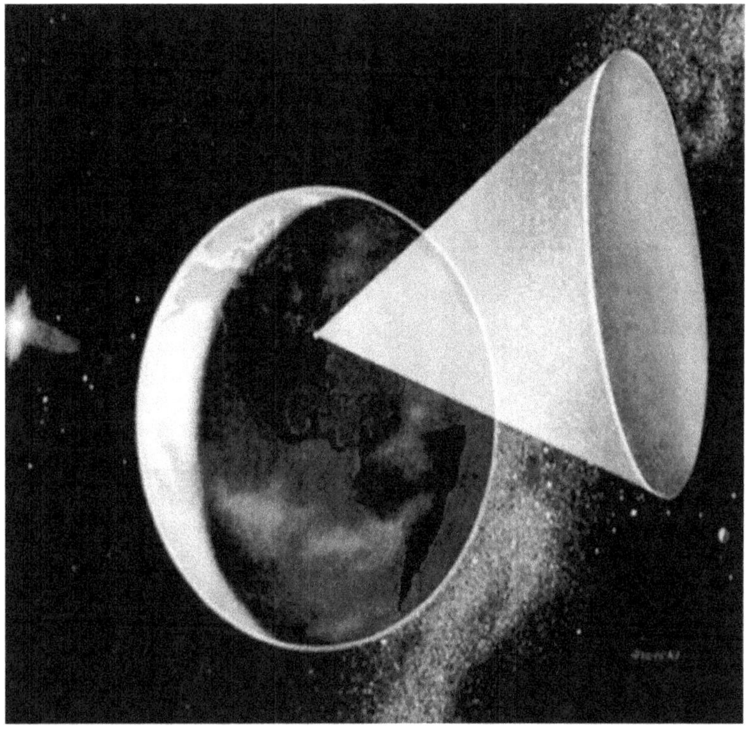

Photo from *Gizmodo.com*

In 1929, a German physicist named Hermann Oberthe developed plans for a space station. His station was to house a 100-meter wide concave mirror which would be used to reflect the sun's light to a concentrated point on earth. Later other German scientists researched his idea and determined that a so-called Sun Gun could be made of metallic sodium reflector and put into orbit at about 5,100 miles. It could be used to reflect the sun's light onto a spot on the earth. It was given the code name Heliobeam.

Germans scientists claimed after the war that the Heliobeam would have been completed within ten years. No prototypes were ever built.

The victorious Allies discovered the plans for the solar cannon in 1945. Detailed research revealed that the super mirror weapon was supposed to orbit the Earth at a distance of about 35,785 kilometers (22,236 miles).

A crewed space station with docking units for supply rockets, oxygen-generating hydroponic gardens, and solar-powered generators were going to form a part of the space mirror. The Allies were astounded by the scale and detailed nature of the plans.[7]

This German secret weapon was far beyond its time but may have laid plans for our orbiting space station of the 20th century.

The Messerschmitt Me 323 Gigant

Me 323 Gigant taking off. Bundesarchiv, Bild 101I-596-0367-5A/Menzendorf

Preparing for Operation Sea Lion; the invasion of England, the German Luftwaffe wanted a large assault glider to carry combat troops in greater numbers. The German Army also wanted it to be able to carry their large 88 millimeters or a Panzer IV tank. Earlier gliders were not large enough so Messerschmitt and Junkers were asked to submit plans for a glider to meet those requirements.

In the meantime, Operation Sea Lion had been canceled but Operation Barbossa; the invasion of Russia, was on and such a glider would be needed. With time as a factor and the decision to use the existing Messerschmitt Me 321 glider. This aircraft had many problems and it was decided to convert it to a motorized six-engine metal propeller blade aircraft that could meet the Luftwaffe and the German army requirements and named the Me323.

The Me323 had a top speed of 136 miles per hour and was armed with five 13 mm machine guns located behind the wings. A pilot, radio operator, engineers, and gunners made up the crew. It was the biggest land-based transport aircraft of World War II.

It first appeared in the Mediterranean in November 1942 to fly supplies to Rommel's Africa forces. A total of 198 Me323 were built before production was stopped in April 1944 because of the direction of the war for Germany. Because it was unpowered it was proposed that it be supplied with six BMW 801 radial air-cooled 14 cylinder engines.

A victory for the Japanese at Midway may have extended the war beyond 1945, the Me323 with new BMW engines may have added to the Luftwaffe and German army another weapon to use again the allies.[8]

The Zielgerät 1229

Photo from *Achtumgpanzer.com*

The first practical night vision devices were developed by the German company AEG (Allgemeine Elektricitäts-Gesellschaft AG "General electricity company") starting in 1935. As early as 1939, the first-night vision devices were introduced by the German army and were used by both tanks and the infantry in World War II.

The ZG 1229 was an infrared device designed to be mounted on various German military weapons. The man-portable system was used by the German infantrymen on the German STG 44 rifle. The STG 44 was a mass-produced assault weapon, designed by the famous small arms designer Hugo Schmeisser and introduced in 1943, renamed the STG 44 in 1944, and called the Vampir. Other smaller infrared devices were introduced in 1944 but the large ZG 1229 wasn't used until February 1945.

Toward the end of World War II, about 50 ZG 1229 were mounted on Mark V Panther tanks and saw action in both the eastern and western fronts.

The ZG 1229 portable Vampir weighed about 5 lbs. and was fitted with lugs at the weapons production facility. For a human target, it had a range of about 100 meters. Night hunter was the name given to soldiers who carried this device.

The searchlight consisted of a conventional tungsten light source shining through a filter permitting only infrared light. The sensor was not sensitive to body heat because it operated in the upper light spectrum rather than in the lower heat spectrum.

Toward the end of the war, the ZG 1229 was effective when used by snipers and similar infrared equipment was mounted on German machine guns. If the war had continued beyond 1945, Germany would have produced more of this type of weapon and greatly affect the war effort.[9]

Fliegerfaust

In 1944 a German metal goods manufacturer named Hasag, also known as Hugo Schneider AG located in Leipzig Germany became a leading Nazi arms-manufacturing company in World War II, developed and built a prototype of an unguided, multi-barreled, man-held portable ground to air rocket launcher designed to destroy enemy ground attack aircraft.

It was designated the Fliegerfaust, also known as the Luftfaust (air fist).

The original design had four 20mm barrels and fired 20mm projectiles by a small rocket with a light load. A later design added five more barrels and increased the length to about 60 inches and the weight to about 14 lbs.

10,000 were ordered in 1945 but only 80 saw actual combat and proved ineffective due to its range.[10]

Credit to Caledonian Dreams/Pinterest

Fliegerfaust Sturmgewehr 44

The Germans invented a weapon that became popular in both World War I and II, the Luger. The standard version was 8.74 inches long, with a barrel length of 4.7 inches, weighing one pound, 15 ounces. What made it an excellent weapon was its firing rate of 116 rounds per minute in its semiautomatic operation and an effective firing range of 56 yards with an eight-round feed system. Well within the regulations of the treaty of Versailles of 1919.

Under the manufacturing regulations of this treaty, Germany was forbidden to develop heavy machine guns but was permitted submachine guns and machine pistols as weapons for their police. This opened the door for a German weapon designer; Hugo Schmeisser, who in the closing months of World War I had designed the Pistole 1918 Bergmann, known as the MP18. The barrel of the MP18 was less than eight inches long and used the chamber for the 9mm rounds which were used in the Luger.

Working around the Treaty of Versailles, Hugo Schmeisser developed his most famous weapon, known as the StG44, it was the first successful assault rifle. It was unique as it included an intermediate cartridge controllable automatic fire with a high rate of fire. Its design was more compact than a standard battle rifle and designed primarily for targets within a few hundred yards. Most infantry rifles were designed to hit targets over a thousand plus yards and the Germans soon learned that they needed a rifle for use in close combat. The StG44 was used successfully on the eastern front against the Russians.

The StG44 was also known as the MP 43 and MP 44 and was a later improvement of earlier designs.[11]

If the war continued beyond 1945, more of these types of weapons would have become available to more German soldiers and could have created more deaths among the Allies' armies.

Sturmgewehr 44

Fieseler Fi 103R

Bundesarchiv, Bild 141-2733/Fotograf(in):o.Ang

Work started early on flying bomb operated by a pulse jet engine. In 1935, a proposal was present to the Luftwaffe for a flying bomb that used a pulse jet engine. The Luftwaffe didn't accept the design or award any production contracts. But it was the start of something to come.

Gerhard Fieseler Werke located in the city of Kassel in northern Germany; was a German aircraft manufacturer in the 1930s and 40s, designed and built the first flying bomb. It was called the Fiesler Fi 103R.

The Fiesler Fi 103R was designed late in the war and never saw combat. It was a flying bomb much like the V-1 but with a pilot. It would be carried below the wings of the Heinkel He 111 bomber and powered by one pulsejet engine which could reach a speed of 497 miles per hour at an altitude of 8,000 feet with a range of 205 miles and carried an explosive warhead of 1874 pounds.

Once released from the bomber, the operation called for the pilot to steer the rocket to the target then bail out before impact but it was normally a suicide mission for the pilots didn't bailout in time. There were no ejection seats. All pilots were volunteers and were required to sign that they knew they may not return.

After a meeting with Hitler on 15 March 1945 in which he was convinced that suicide missions were not part of the German warrior tradition, the program was cancelled.[12]

Although designed late in the war if the Germans had more time; which victory of the Japanese at the Battle of Midway may have given them, the Fiesler Fi 103R may have had ejection seats added and could have been a major problem for Allied forces.

Flettner Fl 282 Kolibri

Photo from *warbirdsresourcegroup.org*

The idea of vertical flight goes back to China in the 400s with their spinning top which became a child's toy. Over the years many attempts were made to have vertical flight but it wasn't till July 1901 that a heavier than air motor drove helicopter by German Hermann Ganswindt took flight in Berlin-Schoneberg carrying humans.[13]

In 1933 German Heinrich Focke at Focke-Wulf was licensed to build the Spanish-designed Cierva C.30 autogyro; which was a design in which the engine was geared directly to drive the rotor blades of the helicopter for take-off. He then designed the world's first practical transverse twin-rotor helicopter as the Focke-Wulf Fw 61 flying for the first time on 26 June 1936. It became the first operation helicopter.[14]

In 1939, Anton Flettner was awarded a contract to produce a different type of helicopter with twin intermeshing rotors set at a slight angle to one another and powered by a single engine. His design was the Flettner FI 265 which flew for the first time in May 1939. It was far superior to the Focke's Fw 61.

A newer version of the FI 265 was introduced in 1940 as the Flettner FI 282 called the Hummingbird helicopter. It was a single-seat helicopter with an open cockpit with one pilot, powered by a 160 HP air-cooled radial piston-driven engine. Max speed of 93 MPH at sea level with a range of about 110 miles.

The German Navy lacking aircraft carriers became interested in the FI 282. They thought that three kinds of helicopters would be needed for the coming war at sea. The German Navy the Kriegsmarine saw the need for a smaller version for shipboard operations, a shore-based one for coastal operations and a mini-helicopter to be carried by submarines.

The Luftwaffe began using the FI 282 for artillery and anti-submarine spotting. They were so impressed with the FI 282 that they ordered 1,000 in 1944. Allied bombers destroyed the plant in Munich and only 24 were built.[15]

The first use of helicopters by the United States in combat was in May 1944.

If the war had continued beyond 1945, more of this type of helicopter would have been produced helping the Nazis to do more damage to Allied forces perhaps changing the outcome of the war.

The Vortex Cannon/Wind Cannon

Photo from pictures *history/2009/10/nazi-secret-weapons-wind-cannon*

Starting in 1942, Austrian Dr. Zippermeyer with his doctorate in engineering opened a research institute with about 35 employees in Vienna and Lower Austria. In his research laboratories near Lofer, Austria, he and his staff worked on trying to duplicate a miniature tornado. Knowing that a natural vortex created a whirlwind by moving particles of air or water would create a spiral around a zone of low pressure.

This research led to the thought that if a physical vortex could be built it might be used as a weapon against enemy aircraft by firing a large mortar with a slow-burning explosive in a shell creating a tornado as it explored around the enemy aircraft destroying the wings of the aircraft. He proceeded to build what he called a vortex cannon to create this tornado in the sky. He first used carbon powder to create the slow-burning explosive. Tests proved that using 60% liquid oxygen mixed with coal dust improved the results. No results were found that indicated this device was successful.

Using this vortex theory, Dr. Zippermeyer had a prototype built by a company in Stuttgart. This model used a mixture of oxygen and hydrogen firing from what he called a wind cannon to destroy enemy aircraft by hitting them with a plug of air. Tests were reported that it could break a one-inch board at a range of 200 meters. This prototype was brought into action as an anti-aircraft defense weapon at the bridge on the Elbe but failed.

As the war was ending further research indicated that a large version of the wind cannon could be produced and may have proven to be successful.[16]

A victory for the Japanese at the Battle of Midway may have delayed the war beyond 1945 and this weapon may have played a bigger role in the results of World War II.

Krummlauf Curved Barrechujkpl

Photo by LIFE Magazine photographer David Scherman in 1945

During the final days of the invasion of Russia, the German soldier was being picked off by Russian snipers whenever they look out to fire their weapon. To help solve this problem the German army came up with a design that could attach to their main rifle, the StG 44 that would allow the weapon to be fired around the corner.

Development of the Krummlauf began in1943 with testing done with a curved 20mm barrel on an 8mm rifle. As development continued bent barrel design at 30, 45, 60, and 90 degree bends were produced. The 30 degree was the only one for the StG 44 that was produced in any number. It would clamp onto the end of the rifle. Due to its design, the 30 degree had a life span of about 300 rounds and the 45 degree of only 160.[17]

Hitler took an immense interest in the Krummer Lauf but it is doubtful if this weapon would have had any effect on the outcome of the war if it continued beyond 1945

The Ruhrstahl X-4

Photo from luft46.com/missile/x-4

Doctor Max Kramer, a German scientist working for Ruhrstahl AG in Germany was responsible for the development and construction of what became known as the Ruhrstahl X-4. He had also done work on one of Germanys' best-known weapons, the Fritz X, the world's first precision-guided weapon.

The German X-4 was a small air-to-air missile that could be fired at Allied bombers from a distance. It used wires running from the missile to the launch aircraft and required the launch pilot to control the missile from released to impact but it couldn't be jammed.

It was a small cigar-shaped body with four sweep wings and four small tail fins. It was powered by a BMW 109-548 liquid-fueled rocket engine. It was constructed of steel, aluminum, and wood, about 6 and one-half feet in length, weighing 90 pounds.

The design was such that unskilled workers could assemble the missile and work began in early 1943 and reached full development by that summer. In August 1944, 225 prototypes had been completed and the first was tested fired on 11 August 1944.

By late 1944 over 1,000 X-4 airframes had been completed waiting for the BMW engines but Allied bombers destroyed the BMW factory, which did not return to production before the war ended.

The X-4 was never issued to the Luftwaffe and didn't see combat.[18]

If the war had continued beyond 1945 and the BMW engine plant could come back online, the Ruhrstahl X-4 may have helped Germany in their war effort.

Die Glocke (The Bell)

This project; if it ever existed, was rumored to have been under the supervision of General Hans Kammler. This SS general played an important part in the complex structure of the Reich's industrial-military complex. Early in his career, he was appointed to the board of directors of the Homeland building and housing cooperative, and when he joined the SS in 1933, he was appointed by Heinrich Himmler to head all construction projects. This position put Kammler in charge of the construction of barracks, total camps and included concentration camps, gas chambers, and crematoria. He was not the operator of these faculties nor did he work on any of these projects, just in charge of the construction. He used slave labor in many of these projects and was known to use extreme brutality and execution to complete his projects on time.[19]

Kammler was later put in charge of building underground facilities for the production of the V2 rockets and the Me 262 jet aircraft. It was rumored that he constructed the faculties that may have worked on an atomic bomb.

As the war was ending; Kammler as a senior member of the SS was listed as a Wanted War Criminal. It was rumored that he committed suicide, his body destroyed, that he was captured by the Americans and he just disappeared. No evidence was ever found that any of these occurred. He remains a man of mystery.

General Hans Kammler may have been in charge of a building where the Bell was to have been built but no evidence supports this theory.

The Bell was to have been a device shaped like a bell containing a liquid, perhaps mercury. The liquid was stored in two cylinders which would spin in opposite directions, emitting blue light. The metal core contained what was called Xerum 525, which was a compound of thorium, beryllium, and mercury.

It was reported that several tests were conducted that required scientists and engineers to wear protective clothing. During one of the early tests, five of the seven scientists involved in the test died. It was suspected that the Bell project resulted in the emission of a considerable amount of radiation.[20]

Once airborne the Bell would appear as a UFO. U.S. Navy pilots reported seen a similar UFO in 2018 over the Atlantic.

Maybe the Bell was real and a forerunner of the UFOs of today.

Feuerball (Fireball)

German aeronautical engineers sought to build several weapons in this so-called class Feuerball. The first, called the Feuerball (Fireball) was designed to interfere with the engines of Allied aircraft. These were silver jet-powered discs that were launched by catapults, remotely controlled by ground operators. It produced an electromagnetic field that was to short circuit the aircraft ignition system which would cause to aircraft to crash. It had a klystron vacuum tubes fitted inside that was designed to jammed Allied aircraft without beginning detected by radar.

When the Feuerball was in flight it would spin on its axis giving a burning appearance, and at night look like a burning ball. Its purpose was to incapacitate the radar of enemy aircraft. They were loaded with a high explosive charge to allow the ground operators to destroy them if there was damage to the guidance system.

The Germans developed a ground equivalent, called the Feuermolch (Fire Salamander). It operated as the Fireball but on the ground in use as artillery. About 50 of these made it to the German front in France.

Another project that came from the Feuerball was the Kugelblitz (Ball Lighting). It was an unmanned jet lift aircraft, shaped like a ball with fused wings, fuselage, and tail formed into a single body. It was designed for vertical takeoff and landing and used an electrostatically fired weapon system with an aerosol gun and television guidance.[21]

Not wanting it to fall into Allied hands it was destroyed in April 1945. If these weapons were ever designed and used, they have had some effect on the war if it was extended beyond 1945.

The Bouncing Bomb

A British engineer named Barnes Wallis began working on plans for a bouncing bomb that could be dropped into the water from an aircraft and skipping along the water it might hit and destroy German ships and dams.

Using this idea, the British Admiralty and the Royal Air Force conducted a test at various sites in England. From these tests, they learned that a 9,000 motorized drum-shaped bomb; which they code-named Upkeep, was best when dropped at a height of 60 feet with a speed of 232 mph. The bomb would spin backward along the surface of the water hitting the dam and the spin would cause it to go down the dam and explore at the base of the dam. The test proved that the best British aircraft for this mission was the Lancaster bombers.

British intelligence revealed that the Germans Mohne dam in Germany's Ruhr valley was heavily used by the Germans for supplying power for many of their war production plants. The British intelligence revealed that three dams were important to the German war production, the Mohne, Edler, and Sorpe.

In late March 1943, the RAF formed a new squadron; code-named Squadron X. On 16 May 1943 at 9:28 pm 19 Lancaster bombers with 133 men took off to attack the three dams, coded named Operation Chastise. The first flight hit Mohne but it wasn't beached, then to Edler which finally collapsed. The two other waves attacked Sorpe, although it was damaged, it remained intact.[22]

The Germans discovered a bounding bomb that failed to explode from a crashed RAF aircraft and reversed engineered it to get their design. The Luftwaffe thought it was a great weapon to use against British shipping and was given the code name Kurt. Having built their version, the Luftwaffe found that the Kurt speed matched the speed of the aircraft delivering it, proving a failure, and discontinued the project in 1944.

Death Ray

The news was spreading in 1935 that Hitler might have a superweapon called a death ray that could incinerate anything including the detonation of a bomb at a long distance.

The British Air Ministry was flooded with letters asking about such a weapon. They asked Scottish physicist Robert Watson Watt; who was a pioneer in radio direction finding and later credited with the invention of radar if such a device was possible. He reported that such a weapon was unlikely.

In the 1930s German scientists developed particle accelerators known as betatrons, which by generating electric fields that will accelerate particles and magnetic fields that steer and focus them. Using this technology, German scientists could create an x-ray weapon.

The Nazi scientists worked toward using these betatrons to turn x-ray beam generators and cannons to fire at approaching aircraft to disable their engines or kill the pilots with blasts of radiation.

Before this type of weapon could be built and tested, American forces captured the plant and prototypes in April 1945. It was reported that one German scientist removed the prototype from the bombed laboratory and turned it over the General Patton's 3rd Army on 14 April 1945.[23]

If the Japanese had won the Battle of Midway and the war continued beyond 1945, this weapon if it could have worked may have had an impact on the war effort for the Germans.

The Ball Tank

World War I known for its No Man's Land issues, raised many concepts of weapons that could deal with such a war. One such concept was the rolling or ball tank. The German company Hansa-Lloyd Werke A.G. in Bremen, Germany tried to produce a prototype called the Treffas-Wagen in 1917. It was believed to be a one-man scouting machine. It had only 5 mm armor and little firepower. On 14 May 1917, a demonstration was conducted and after several tests, the German Supreme Army Command rejected the design and stated it was unfit for combat.

The lack of success in World War I didn't keep the Germans from trying again for such a weapon in World War II known as the Kugelpanzer, which translates to Ball Tank. It was manufactured by the German company Krupp. Little is known of the weapon but the Soviets found one at the end of the war in Manchuria. It had been stripped of most of its inside and without any documentation. It was suspected that the Germans had shipped one to the Japanese. It appeared to be a one-person light reconnaissance tank with a small motor and wheel on the rear to aid in steering.

Nothing is known of its use in combat and no other prototypes were found.[24]

Chapter 12
Atomic Bomb Program

"It was rightly feared that if the war in the West were unduly prolonged, German scientists would invent secret weapons that would prove irresistible… There was no time to lose in eliminating German science from the war. There was no comparable peril from Japanese science." American historian Samuel Eliot Morison responds to the question asked about what would have happened if World War II had been prolonged.[1]

Historian Morison was correct about his statement of the fear of World War II had gone beyond 1945. Not only did Germany have some of the best or perhaps the best scientists in the world but the Nazis would have likely used any weapon their scientists could have invented to win the war, even the atomic bomb.

Nazi Germany's propaganda ministry assigned the term Wunderwaffe (Wonder Weapon) to their superweapons. These advanced weapons required long periods of design and testing before if any had the merit to be brought into action. If the war had lasted longer some might have developed to the point that they could have affected the outcome of the war. Such was the Panther tank and the Type XXI submarine. If the Germans had more time both the Panther tank and the Type XXI submarine could have become a better weapon for the Germans. With the defeat of Germany appearing on the horizon, the Germans rushed both of these weapons into production resulting in poor performance in the field. If the war had continued beyond 1945, these two weapons could have affected the outcome of the war.

Some of the designs were developed further after the war by the allies and did have an impact on future weapons.

The Germans had eight other designs that could have caused problems for the Allies if the war had lasted longer than 1945. These eight were discussed in the previous chapter but the two most important and which could have affected the outcome of the war if it had lasted longer based on the Japanese winning at the Battle of Midway are discussed now in more detail.

Atomic Bomb

Albert Einstein wrote President Roosevelt in August 1939, "that it may become possible to set up a nuclear chain reaction in a large mass of uranium by which vast amounts of power and large quantities of new radium-like elements would be generated. Now it appears almost certain that this could be achieved in the immediate future. This phenomenon would also lead to the construction of bombs, and it is conceivable—though much less certain—that extremely powerful bombs of a new type may thus be constructed..."[2].

In the 5th century BC, the Greeks knew that all matter was composed of indivisible building blocks and they called these particles atoms; which meant indivisible, from which we get atoms. The ancient Greeks first proposed that all matter in the universe is constant. This resulted in that law of conservation of matter in physic in the 18th century. That is that matter cannot be created or destroyed within an isolated system. It means that in a chemical reaction the mass of the products will always be equal to the mass of the reactants. This understanding of the atom and how it acts laid the groundwork that was to follow leading to the atomic and nuclear bomb.[3]

Ernest Rutherford working in the Cavendish Laboratory at the University of Cambridge in England discovered the atomic nucleus in 1911 and observed its proton in 1919. He thought that there must be something in the nucleus in addition to the protons. In 1920, he proposed that an electron and a proton could combine to form a new, neutral particle. But he wasn't able to prove it.

In 1913 the Danish physicist Niels Bohr presented the first theoretical model; which became known as the Bohr Model. Doctor Bohr found that electrons in atoms travel in defined circles around the central nucleus. Similar to how planets orbit around our sun.

His description of the structure of atoms, especially that of hydrogen described the properties of atomic electrons in terms of a set of allowed values. This resulted in understanding that atoms absorb or emit radiation only when the electrons abruptly jump. This was another major step toward the development of the bomb.

James Chadwick; an English physicist educated at the University of Manchester, began to work on his master's degree in the Cavendish Laboratory with Rutherford. While he worked on other projects, he continued to work on radioactivity. He became aware of work in this field by a couple of German physicists and he was convinced of the existence of the neutron. He published a paper in May 1932 titled "Existence of a Neutron." He received the Nobel Prize in 1935 for his discovery of the neutron, paving the way for the atom bomb.

Over Christmas 1938, two physicists, Lise Meitner, and her nephew Otto Frisch had discovered something previously thought impossible but was happening: that a uranium nucleus had split in two and nuclear fission was born. The path to an atom bomb was clear.

Shortly after German scientists Otto Hahn and Fritz Strassmann inadvertently discovered fission; Germany formed a secret nuclear weapon program on 1 September 1939, the day that Germany invaded Poland, starting World War II. The program was called Uranverein (the Uranium Club).[4]

The Germans had a head start over other countries because of their strong industrial base, a group of the best scientists in the world, and a military that was interested in new technology that could be used for military purposes.

The German Army Ordnance had a keen interest in this program because of its' promise of being of military value and took over the program. They held their first meeting in Berlin on 16 September 1939 attending were a select group of key leaders in this field. Another meeting was held shortly after the first adding additional experts in this area including Werner Karl Heisenberg, a theoretical physicist and a key pioneer in quantum mechanics was invited. He had received the Nobel Prize in Physics in 1932.[5]

In Niels Bohr's theory of the atom, electrons absorb and emit radiation of fixed wavelengths when jumping between fixed orbits around a nucleus. The theory provided a good description of the spectrum created by the hydrogen atom but needed to be developed to suit more complicated atoms and molecules. In 1925, Werner Heisenberg formulated a type of quantum mechanics based on matrices. In 1927 he proposed the "uncertainty relation", setting limits for how precisely the position and velocity of a particle can be simultaneously determined.[6]

Dr. Heisenberg in 1942 at a scientific conference call by the Army Weapons Office, gave a lecture entitled "The theoretical basis for energy generation from uranium fission." His lecture was about the energy potential of nuclear fission. He spoke that pure U-235 had to be obtained to achieve a chain reaction.

On 4 June 1942, Heisenberg, reported to Albert Speer; Germany's Minister of Armaments, on the prospects for converting uranium research into the development of a nuclear weapon. Dr. Heisenberg told him that a bomb could not be developed before 1945 because it would require lots of monetary resources and many scientists. He did state to the Danish physicist Niels Bohr according to Bohr son, Aage Bohr that he, Heisenberg thought the new possibilities could decide the outcome of the war if the war dragged on.[7]

Dr. Werner Karl Heisenberg gave many talks on his theory of energy generation from uranium fission and from 24 January to 4 February 1944 he traveled to occupied Copenhagen and spoke there. In April he lectured in neutral Switzerland while there the United States Office of Strategic Services sent; the forerunner of the Central Intelligence Agency sent an agent named Moe Berg; who had been an average major league catcher but became a spy in World War II, to attend the lecture carrying a pistol and was instructed to shoot Heisenberg if his lecture indicated that Germany was close to achieving an atomic bomb. Heisenberg did not reveal anything about the Nazis having an atomic bomb during the lecture. Later Moe Berg was able to meet Dr. Heisenberg at dinner and after listening carefully to conversations with Dr. Heisenberg, there was no indication that Germany was working on an atomic bomb.[8]

The Germans had other higher priorities which required their resources as the war dragged on and Albert Speers was aware of these. The thought within the German military research was that their current demand for raw materials and scientists for the war now did not justify spending time on this research unless there is a certainty of getting some benefit from it soon. [9]

Historians continue to debate what would have happened had the Germans invested significant resources in their nuclear program, and if it could have changed the outcome of the war.

According to Rainer Karlsch in his book, "Hitler Bombe", if the Germans had a tactical nuclear weapon, its potential for destruction was far below that of the two American atomic bombs and were tested successfully several times shortly before the end of the war. Karlsch said in his book. "What Nazi Germany lacked was enough fissile material such as enriched uranium to make a full-size, functioning the Nazis conducted crude nuclear experiments, but Karlsch said he has discovered additional evidence, notably in the archives of the former Soviet Union. The book cites postwar witness accounts and Soviet military intelligence reports to back up its theory of a March 3, 1945, experimental nuclear test blast at the Nazis' Ohrdruf military testing area then run like a concentration camp by the Nazi SS but offers no firsthand documentary proof."

Many reports have come from sources in the Russian military that they had information from a German informant that a blast was conducted by the Germans which could have been from an atomic bomb test but no reliable evidence has ever been submitted that such a test took place.

The possibility of the Germans working on an atomic weapon came to the U.S. attention when many refugees from Germany before the war broke out revealed that they had studied under the Germans before the war started and on an atomic program. Robert Furman; who was working on the United States Manhattan Project, was reported to have said that that Project was built on fear that the Germans had the bomb. The Chief of Foreign Intelligence for the Manhattan Project, General Leslie Groves had said, "Unless and until we had positive knowledge to the contrary, we have to assume that the most competent German scientists and engineers were working on an atomic program with the full support of their government and with the full capacity of German Industry at their disposal. Any other assumption would have been unsound and dangerous."

The research found that heavy water was a key to making the bomb and with Germany's invasion of Norway in 1940; we knew that they now had control of the Norsk Hydro heavy water plant at Vemork in Norway. Now Germany had a heavy water plant under its control.

If the invasion of France in 1944 had been delayed, would Germany have had time to get the bomb?

Chapter 13
Germany's Rocket Program

The German rocket program had its founding in the Verein fur Raumschiffahrt, referred to as the VfR. It was formed on 5 June 1927 in Breslau, the largest city east of Berlin. One of its prominent members was Hermann Oberth, the leading German expert of rocketry. At its peak, it had over 500 members.

Oberth had designed a liquid-fueled rocket motor and conducted a static firing in the fall of 1929. He was aided in this work by a young 18-year-old named Wernher von Braun, who would become a leader in rocketry in his own right.[1]

The Treaty of Versailles forbid Germany to have an air force, but rockets were not banned, probably because none had been used in warfare and little was known about them at that time. The VfR was allowed to build and test rockets. The first test of a rocket powered by a mixture of petrol and liquid oxygen was in August 1930. The rocket was called the Mirak-1 and the test was a success but later tests failed due to the liquid oxygen tank bursting to cause the rocket to explode.

As future work on rockets was met with success, the German military took over the rocket program, and the VfR dissolved in 1934 as Wernher von Braun joined the military rocket program and started working on many types of rockets, the most successful being the V-2.[1]

The RAF and the American bombers were having success in attacking German cities in 1943 and the Germans began work on a weapon that was planned to be able to have the range to hit allied attack aircraft from a great distance. This is why the X-4 Ruhrstahl discussed earlier was designed to hit the attack bombers before they were over the German cities. Its rocket engine could reach speeds over 700 mph with a 45 lb. fragmentation bomb. It was first launched on 11 August 1944 but problems with the design were not worked out till 1945 as a production of 1,000 was started. Because of the end of the war, none of the X-4 was any action. If the invasion of France had been delayed due to the Japanese victory at Midway, the X-4 weapon may have helped Germany to defeat the Allies.

The Germans never saw the value of their rockets and giving them the funding they needed until it was too late in the war. This may have been because of Hitler's lack of knowledge of rockets until he saw the success of the V-1 and V-2 against England. If their rocket program had been at the head of their military funding, the result of the war may have been different if it continued beyond 1945.

V-1 Rocket

Bundesarchiv, Bild 146-1975-117-26 / Fotograf(in): Lysiak, Bruno

V-2 Rocket

Bundesarchiv, RH8II Bild-D06-44 / Fotograf(in): o.Ang.

One of the most important of all the German weapons was the rockets coming out of this project. In the 1930s, even before Hitler became well known, the German Army Weapons Agency was working on a rearmament program and it was assigned to the German Army Acceptance Organization. By 1940 it had over 25,000 men to assist the inspection of the rearmament weapons. The German Army Weapons Agency established a unit specially charged with developing rockets to be used for military purposes. It was established at an army base in the German small-town of Kummersdorf about 60 miles south of Berlin. General Walter Dornberger, an artillery officer in World War I and one of the few German officers to stay in the small German army that was allowed after that war. The army sent him in 1925 to the School of Technology in Charlottenberg, west of Berlin. While where he specialized in ballistics and was assigned to the development of rocket weapons, which were not prohibited by the Treaty of Versailles.

General Dornberger was assigned as the head of the rocket program at Kummersdorf, a city about 16 miles south of Berlin. Kummersdorf was the location of the German Army weapon office at that time. He was looking for a design of a liquid-fueled long-range military rocket. It was during this time that General Dornberger recruited Wernher von Braun. A name that would appear again and again in both German and American rocket development.[2]

As the rocket projects got larger it outgrew the facility at Kummersdorf and in 1937, the German Army Weapon Office opened the Peenemunde Army Research Center on the northern peninsula of the Baltic island of Usedom between Germany and Poland. It was called the HVP short for the German name of the center. Five different military proving and testing grounds were located in this area.[3]

On 25 September 1942, Goering authorized the development of four types of surface-to-air missiles: unguided rockets called Taifun, target-seeking guided rockets called Enzian; operator optically-guided rockets named Rheintochter and Schmetterling; and radar-guided rockets named Wasserfal.

The Taifun, German for the typhoon, was an unguided rocket that was to be launched in mass waves at Allied bombers. They were small and cheap to build. Production was started in January 1945 with plans to build 10,000 only 600 were complete by the end of the war.

They were never deployed, although after the war the U.S. used its design for one of its rockets.[4]

The Enzian was guided by a ground operator, using a built-in guidance system. It was intended to destroy multiple Allied bombers as it explored when in close contact with many bombers flying in formation. Several were built but proved unsuccessful as the rocket flew faster than the ground operator could control.[5]

Rheintochter and Schmetterling, both of these were TV-guided German surface-to-air missile projects developed during World War II. There was also an air-to-air version. The operator used a telescopic sight and a joystick to guide the missile by radio control. The test for both of these weapons was successful and they were put into production but as the end of the war was approaching, both projects were canceled. Rheintochter is German for Rhine Maiden and Schmetterling is Buttefly.[6]

If the war had continued beyond 1945, both of these weapons may have played a bigger role in the outcome of the war.

Due to the increased Allied bombing raids, the Germans looked for different ways was to bring down Allied bombers. Luftwaffe fighters and antiaircraft guns were effective but costly in pilots and aircraft lost, plus the amount of ammunition required was costly at this stage of the war. The Germans started work on project Wasserfall (Waterfall) in 1941, it was a variant of the V2 rocket but designed as an anti-aircraft weapon. It was a supersonic surface-to-air missile, smaller than the V2, and used a shorter launch trajectory. Controlled by a manual radio guidance system, which worked perfectly in the daytime but not at night.

Finally, the Germans came up with a system for night operations using radar to track the enemy aircraft. But the key person in the design of this project. Dr. Thiel was killed during a British bombing attack in August 1943. His death and other problems caused the Wasserfall never to be deployed in combat.[7]

If the Germans had more time to solve the problems with this Weapon, the Wasserfall may have helped their war efforts against the Allies.

V-1

Finally, after many changes were made to the V-1 design, the Luftwaffe accepted the V-1 for a weapon of great use again the enemy. It went into production and was given the codename Kirschkery (Cherry Stone). The fuselage was constructed mainly of welded sheet steel with wings of plywood, was about 25 feet long with a wingspan of about 20 feet. It was powered by a pulsejet engine that pulsed 50 times per second. It carried an 1870 pound warhead at about 360 miles per hour and was called a buzz bomb or doodlebug due to the noise it created once in the air. The pulse jet engine required airflow for ignition so it couldn't operate below 150 miles per hour. The Germans designed a ground catapult that would boost the rocket to 200 miles per hour at launch allowing the pulse jet engine to ignite. It could then obtain speeds up to 400 miles per hour, allowing the range to increase more than the 150 miles. Once it was launched its direction couldn't be controlled.[8]

The Peenemunde site became the center for all German rocket research, development, and production. It also produced its liquid oxygen and wind tunnel. On the western side of this facility, the V-1 flying bomb was worked on by the German air force. The eastern side was where work on the V-2 rocket was conducted under the eye of Wernher von Braun. The V-1 was a subsonic, short-range, non-controllable pilotless missile or rocket. The Germans developed 138 rocket models but the best was the V-2 rocket.[9]

Credit: By Spike78 - Own work, CC BY-SA 4.0,
https://commons.wikimedia.org/w/index.php

The Aggregat series was a set of rocket designs that Nazi Germany's army developed in 1933-45.[10]

A-1 Rocket (1933)

The A-1 was the first in this series. It was designed in 1933 by the soon to become famous Wernher von Braun in the German armed forces research program at Kummersdorf, run by Walter Dornberger. The A-1 was the grandfather of modern rockets. It was 4 ft 7 inches long, 12 inches in diameter with a takeoff weight of 331 lbs. The engine used a pressure-fed rocket propellant system burning alcohol and liquid oxygen, producing 660 lbs. of thrust for 16 seconds. It was stabilized by an 88 lb. three-axis gyroscope system in the nose.

The engine had been tested but the first flight attempt blew up on the launch pad in December 1933 a half-second after ignition. Due to the design proving to be unstable no further tests were conducted and a new design was started on what would be called the A-2. The A-1 was nose heavy and with the A-2 the gyroscope was moved to the middle of the rocket.

A-2 Rocket (1934)

The A-2 had the same dimensions as the A-1 and the same 660 thrust engine but separate propellant tanks. It used a mushroom-shaped injector system consisting of fuel and oxidizer jets pointing at one another. The propellants were pressurized via a nitrogen tank.

Static tests were conducted in October 1934. Two were built for a full test and were launched before German top army brass on Borkum Island in the North Sea on 19 and 20 December 1934. The first obtained an altitude of 1.4 miles and the second 2.2 miles.

A-3 Rocket (1935-1937)

The plans for the A-3 rocket called for an inertial guidance system with a 3,300 lb. thrust engine. Two new test stands were approved at Kummersdorf including mobile test rigs, small locomotives, office, and storage space in 1935, and the A-3 design was launched.

In March 1936 a static firing of the engine for the A-3 was observed by Army brass and was successful. The A-3 used the same pressure-fed propellant system that was used on the A-1 and A-2. Its design was larger than the other two rockets, 22 feet long, 2.3 feet in diameter, and weighing 1650 pounds when fully fueled. Fins were added to provide arrow stability as its design was based on the eight-millimeter infantry bullet. Pitch and yaw gyros were added to provide better flight. The engine was a scaled-up version of the A-2 using alcohol spraying up to mix with the oxygen being sprayed down, this allowed for better mixing and generated a higher burning temperature.

The first A-3 was launched on 4 December 1937 from the new testing center at the Peenemunde area. The parachuted deployed prematurely, the engine failed and it crashed close to the takeoff point. A second launch occurred on 6 December 1937 with similar results. Additional launches were conducted without success but one did reach a downrange distance of 7.5 miles at an altitude of 11 miles. Due to the failures the A-3 was abandoned and work on the A-4 was postponed and the A-5 was started for research only.

A-5 Rocket (1938-1942)

The A-5 started as a research project to try different parts to solve the problems that were on the A-2 and A-3. They changed the electrical carriages, the jet vane control servomotors to control the pitch, roll, and yaw. A new designed guidance and control system, designed by Siemens was used. The rocket motor was the same as the A-3. The overall length was the same as the A-3 but the diameter was 2.5 feet.

The parachute recovery system which was a problem on the A-3 was redesigned and could stay afloat in water for up to two hours. It was painted yellow and red to allow for easy location and recovery. The internal vanes in the A-3 were made of molybdenum; they were changed to graphite in the A-5. Uncontrolled A-5s were launched in the autumn of 1938 and models of five feet long and eight inches in diameter were dropped from the He-111 bomber in September 1938.

Changes were made to the A-5 and successful flights were conducted in October 1939. The A-5 was now 19.11 ft long, 2ft 7 inches in diameter with a takeoff weight of 2,000 lbs. Further test launches were made resulting in reaching a height of 7.5 miles and a range of 11 miles.

It became clear that von Braun's rocket designs were turning into useful German weapons. By 1941 about 70 A-5 rockets had been fired and up to 80 launches were conducted by October 1943.

After the testing was complete, Dr. Dornberger said, "I now knew that we should succeed in creating a weapon with far greater range than any artillery. What we had successfully done with the A-5 must be equally valid, in improved form for the A-4."

A-4 V-2 (1942-1945)

Work on the A-4 had been postponed while the A-5 was solving problems that had occurred with the A-3. Now that the A-5 was proven to have solved most of these problems, the A-4 was back.

The full-size A-4 design had a range of 200 miles with a peak altitude of 55 miles carrying a payload of one ton of explosives. It became the first ballistic missile and the first projectile to reach outer space. It was propelled with liquid oxygen, 75% ethyl alcohol, and 25% water mixture, about the same as the A-5.

Dr. Domberger; head of research, seeing the success of the A-5 and the A-4 moved the center to a more secure location at Peenemunde on the island Usedom on Germany's Baltic coast where the test could be fired into the sea. The first firing of the A-4 was in March 1942. It flew about one mile before crashing into the sea. The second launch reached about 7 miles before exploding. On 3 October 1942, a third firing occurred reaching an altitude of 52 miles and landed 120 miles away. A highly successful test and production started in 1943.

In late 1943, ideas were presented and call the A-4 SLM. The proposal was for a towable watertight container that could hold an A-4 rocket. It would be towed behind a U-boat and when in a firing position, would rise to a vertical firing position. By the end of the war, one example had been completed but the war ended before it could be tested in combat.

If the war had continued beyond 1945, this weapon could have been used to attack the east of the United States.

The A-4 was given its' name by the German Army Ordnance but when the Nazi Propaganda Ministry saw the success of the rocket as a weapon and took control, they named it the V-2 when it was publicly announced in November 1944.

As the war progressed and German forces were moving back toward Germany, the brains behind the rocket programs knew that their rockets would have to travel further to reach targets in England. The German scientists; such as von Braun, would need their A-4 rocket to travel a longer distance. As they began to develop this idea, it became known as the A-9 and A-4b. They kept the name A-4 because it had received national priority and funds would be available to continue the project.

To increase the range of the A-4/A-9 wings were fitted to the body of the rocket, increasing its range to 470 miles, allowing it to hit targets in England. The first test was done on 27 December 1944 and a failure. A second test was done on 24 January 1945 was partially successful as the wing broke off. It did break the sound barrier and achieved Mach 4.

Remember that the A-4 under the Nazi Propaganda Ministry was the popular V-2.

The V–2 rocket was the world's first long-range ballistic missile, and it comprised five major subassemblies: warhead, control compartment, midsection, propulsion unit, and tail unit. The 2,200-pound warhead consisted of 550 pounds of warhead casing and 1,650 pounds of explosive. The warhead used an impact-detonating two-fuse system that withstood the six-g acceleration and vibration of powered flight. The powerful explosive had to be insensitive to the heat and shock of flight. A piloted V–1 rocket was designed but never used in combat.

Interception of the long-range V-2 was virtually impossible because as the rocket ran out of fuel it would go into an almost vertical drive.[11]

Rockets Planned but not constructed A-6

A proposal was submitted for a manned aerial reconnaissance version of the A-4b. It would be launched vertically by a rocket taking it to a height of 59 miles. It would fall, re-entering the atmosphere in a supersonic glide phase, when its ramjet engine would ignite. This would allow it to stay airborne 15 to 20 minutes and obtaining a speed of 1800 mph. The A-6 would return to its base and land, available to fly again.

The German Air Ministry rejected the proposal and the project ended.

A-7

Between 1940 and 1943 a winged design was developed, named the A-7 for the Kriegsmarine, the German navy. It was similar to the A-5 but had larger tail unit fins to gain greater range in a gliding flight.

Two unpowered models were built and dropped from airplanes to test their flight stability. No powered models were ever tested and the project was canceled.

A-8

The A-8 was a short-lived proposed stretched version of the A-4 using storable rocket propellants. It never entered the prototype phase.

A-9 A-10

Design started in 1940 for a two-stage missile for transatlantic travel, called the A9/A10. It was to be the first world's practical transatlantic ballistic missile and designed to hit the United States. It was estimated that the launch time would be in 1946.

To obtain the distance to reach the United States it had to be a multi-stage missile. The first stage was the A10 and used a multi-chamber design which had a group of six of the A-4 combustion chambers feeding a single expansion nozzle, producing 200 metric tons of thrust. Test stands were built at the Peenemunde site for firing the engine.

The second stage in the original design was called the A-9 and was based on the A-4 with swept wings. Later this stage was changed by adding two fuselage strakes; which are small blade-like devices mounted on the missile, enhancing the aerodynamics by directing the airflow at specific angles of attack, creating less drag on the missile. The second stage was placed in the forward inter-stage of the A-10.

The A9/A10 was 134 ft tall and 13.51 ft in diameter, designed to carry a payload of 2,200 lbs. with a thrust of 449,600 lbs., carrying a gross mass of 188,000 lbs.

The test proved that the guidance system was inaccurate for the planned range for the A9/A10. It was decided that the A-9 would have to be piloted. The design called for the A-9 to reach an altitude of 24 miles before the engine cut off, it would then re-enter the atmosphere and begin a long glide to extend the range. At this point, the pilot would be guided by signals sent from German U-boats on the surface of the Atlantic Ocean. Once the pilot reached the target, he would lock on the site, before ejecting. The chance of surviving was narrow.

Nazi Germany shifted all efforts to the A-4/V-2 rocket due to its success against England resulting in all work on the A9/A10 not being allowed after 1943. Knowing the importance of the A9/A10, Von Braun continued to spend time perfecting and producing the weapon under the cover name of the A4b rocket design.

The invasion at Normandy in June 1944 brought the full force of the United States against Germany and proved that the Nazis need a weapon that would do damage to the United States. In late 1944, the work on A9/A10 resumed under the code name Projekt Amerika (Project America). Due to the allies bombing, no improvements were possible for changes to the system hardware and the project ended after the last test in January 1945.

If the war had continued beyond 1945, the A9/A10 may have brought the United States to the peace tables with Germany.

A-11

Seeing the need to get the A9/A10 into orbit, cross the Atlantic Ocean and reach the United States, Von Braun designed another stage to the A9/A10 called the A11. This would be the first of three stages to the A9/A10. It would use six of the large single chambers engines as the A10. The second stage would be a modification of the A10 within the A11. The A9 was to be the third stage. This would allow a payload of about 660 lbs. in a low orbit of the earth.

A-12

Desiring to get a heavier payload into orbit, Von Braun was designing a true orbital rocket by creating the fourth stage. This would comprise the A9, A10, A11, and the new stage the A12. His calculations showed a possible payload of 10 tons.

The war ended before any of the designs for the A9, A10, A11, or A12 were placed together to create the first true intercontinental missile.[12]

The leading figure of the V-2 rocket program was Dr. Wernher von Braun, who General Dornberger had brought into the rocket program. Dr. von Braun became interested in space when he received a telescope at the age of thirteen. He became a member of a German Amateur Rocket Society known as the VfR. In the spring of 1932, this society held a launch of rockets and von Braun stood out. General Dornberger was present at that event and offered the young von Braun an opportunity to develop his rocket and be paid by the Army. After obtaining his doctors in 1934 at just 22 years of age, he began to work for the army on various rocket programs which would lead to the V-2 rocket. While working on the V-2 rocket program, von Braun joined the Nazi Party and became a member of the SS. Regardless of all the work he did and would do for the American Space Program this decision haunted him.[13]

Dr. von Braun estimated that over 65 modifications were made to the V-2 before it was ready for mass production. It was a liquid-fueled long-range military rocket, designed at a high speed at 3600 miles per hour, traveling at nearly five times the speed of sound. It was a controllable weapon that could carry a heavy destructive load of up to 2200 pounds. It was 46 feet tall, 23 tons in weight, a range over 180 miles, and could reach a height of 6 miles vertically then proceed on an arced course until its fuel ran out. Out of fuel the missile would tip over and fall on its target reaching a speed of close to 4,000 mph. The force of the impact was so much that the missile would burrow itself into the ground several feet before exploding. Once it was in the air, there was no defense against it. It was once test-fired straight up reaching 128 miles.

On 3 October 1942 the V-2 rocket missile; the brainchild of rocket scientist Wernher von Braun, was successfully test-fired from Peenemunde, an island off Germany's Baltic coast. It traveled 118 miles with a one-ton payload.[14]

From Peenemunde, rockets could be test-fired into the open sea without being detected. It was a well-kept secret location and was not detected by the Allies until 1944.

Albert Speer, the Germany Minister of Armaments and War Production upon seeing and inspecting the V-2 said, "It was like the planning of a miracle."[15]

Only after the Battle of Britain in 1940, did Hitler admit the British air superiority that he turned toward giving the rocket program top priority. Now that Germany had conquered France, Hitler approved a plan to begin construction of bunkers in France from which both the V-1 and V-2 rockets could be fired toward England. After seeing how successful the German rockets were, Hitler claimed, "If we'd had these rockets in 1939 we'd never have had this war."[16]

Seeing how successful both the V-1 and V-2 were at hitting England, the British Air Force on locating the German facility at Peenemunde began bombing raids. Thousands of slaves were working at the Peenemunde site and many were killed along with scientists, other workers as well as buildings and rocket sites in these raids which were mostly conducted at night.

Because of these bombing raids, the Germans decided to move the complete works at Peenemunde to underground caverns at Nordhausen along the Zorge River on the southern slopes of the Harz Mountains in central Germany. This was a high mountain area for their rockets with over 800 acres. While rocket production moved from Peenemunde to Nordhausen, testing and rocket firing was moved to a site in Poland while research was underground in parts of Germany and Austria.[17]

In 1944, the Germans set up the V-2 in Holland using mobile launchers in a small clearing, taking only about an hour to prepare and fire the missile. Because the missile sites were portable they were hard to locate before they fired. They were placed under the control of the SS and two missiles were fired at Paris on 6 September 1944. Two were fired at London on 8 September 1944 and followed by more than 1100 through March 1945. It is estimated that more than 2,700 died in England from the V-2 Missile attacks.

Speaking to those working on the V-2 rocket at Peenemunde on 3 October 1942, General Dornberger said, "This is the first of a new era in transportation that of space travel. So long as the war lasts; our most urgent task can only be the rapid perfection of the rocket as a weapon. The development of possibilities we cannot yet envisage will be a peacetime task." [18]

It appears from this statement that the General knew the value of the German rocket research for peacetime work which he would assist when he came to America after the war.

In 1943, the Germans designed and tested a simpler and scaled-down version of the V2. It was a short-range missile named the Rheinbote (Rhine Messenger). It was the only missile of its type used during the war. Its range less than 100 miles but with speed up to 4,200 mph, to an altitude up to 256,000 ft and could carry an 88 lb. warhead. Over 200 were fired at Antwerp as the Germans retreated from Belgium in 1944 during the battle of the Bulge. At the end of the war, the Soviets captured the plans to the Rheinboto. [19]

In 1940, Germany began to develop a two-stage transatlantic ballistic missile, designated the A9/10. At their sites in Germany and Austria work was done on this intercontinental missile; called the Amerika Rocket designed to reach New York City, Washington, D.C., or any other large east coast city in the United States in 40 minutes carrying a warhead. Records discovered after the war revealed that the Germans had placed a high priority on the development of a rocket/missile that could hit the United States and that the rocket was practically complete at the end of March 1945. [20]

If the records on the A9/10 discovered after the war did indicate how close the Germans were to an intercontinental missile that could hit the United States and the war had lasted longer than 1945, a Japanese victory at the Battle of Midway may have given the Germans a strong chance to have changed the results of World War II.

General Dornberger's memoirs stated that they were testing a two-stage rocket with the top stage called the A-4 on the Amerika Rocket A-10 that would separate over the Atlantic Ocean and the upper stage continued with payload to the United States target.

It had a payload of 2,200 lbs. with a thrust of almost 450,000 lb./ft, weighing 188,000 lbs. It was 134 ft tall with a diameter of 13.51 ft. It was a big, heavy weapon. [21]

As work continued on this project, the first stage called the A10 used a multi-chamber design, later changed to a massive single chamber. The second stage named the A9 originally had swept wings, later was changed to a two fuselage ridge to give better aerodynamic stability. Work on the A9/10 was suspended in 1943 to shift more efforts to the V-2 rocket production and its success against London. Von Braun did continue some work on the A9/10 project till it was re-started in 1944. Test stands were built at Peenemunde that allowed the A9/10 to be test-fired.

The end of the war stopped the A9/10 project but it was known that Dr. von Braun had sketched out future changes to the missile to include adding a stage called the A11, which would allow for a satellite launch. He had also planned another stage called the A12, which would result in a four-stage vehicle placing the A9 in a manned orbital space shuttle.

Silverbird

Another way to build a bomber that could attack the United States was being designed by a young Austrian aerospace engineer named Eugen Sanger, born in Bohemia and attending the Graz University of Technology in Austria. He trained as a civil engineer but after reading The Rocket into Interplanetary Space by Hermann Oberth in 1923, he switched his studies to aeronautics.

In 1933 he published a book entitled Rakentenflugtechnik (Rocket Flight Engineering). This work was the first treatise by an academic professional on rocketry and the study of the concept of space planes. In October of that year, he proposed to the Austrian army the development of a rocket-powered hypersonic bomber. Later in that year, he began to test rocket engines. But the Austrian Defense Ministry rejected his proposal.

In 1935 he published articles on a rocket-powered flight for the Austrian journal Flug (Flying). These attracted the attention German Air Ministry, which saw Sänger's ideas as a potential way to accomplish the goal of building a bomber that could strike the United States.

In 1936, Sänger accepted a position from the German High Command to be head of the development center for jet engines in Trauen, Germany. Later a young physicist, Irene Bredt joined him as an assistant. Her activities became thermodynamic and gas kinetics problems related to liquid-propelled rockets.

The Germans set up a secret aerospace research institute within the development center for Sanger and his assistance Bredt.

He developed a concept of a vehicle that could be propelled into the upper atmosphere, glide without power until it descended into dense air. Once in the denser air, its kinetic energy would allow it to skip off the atmosphere back up to higher altitudes. It would repeat this until the energy was reduced then when exhausted it would fall toward its target.

Working there with his assistant Irene Bredt, they designed a manned, winged vehicle with a flat bottom, low-aspect-ratio wing, slick designed and fueled by liquid rocket engine that could reach orbit then descend back into the atmosphere, he called it his Silverbird. Its designed range was such that it would be able to reach the United States. It became known as the Amerika Bomber. He calculated that to get to the United States his plane would need three skips along the atmosphere before heading to the target.

During World War II, Sanger continued his research which included designs of combustion chambers with thrust up to 100 tons, jet propulsion, and constructed ramjet engines. Continuing to work with Irene Bradt they had the final design of the Amerika Bomber, which they called the Sanger-Bredit Antipodal Bomber in August 1944, too late in the war to play an important role.

Once again many German secret weapons were close to being built that could have changed the outcome of the war if they had more time. A victory of the Japanese at the Battle of Midway may have given them more time.

The German Air Ministry in January 1942 issued a requirement for a long-range operational aircraft with a hefty bomb load, to be used as a bomber or reconnaissance duty. An engineer at Focke-Wulfs working for a German manufacturer of civilian and military aircraft, released plans for a large aircraft, with six radial piston engines located on a straight monoplane wing. It was called the Ta 400.

The Ta 400 was designed for a crew of nine with one remote-controlled turret under the fuselage and two remote-controlled turrets on the upper fuselage and a remote-controlled turret in the tail. All were 20 mm cannons. It had a range of 7,500 miles with a bomb load of 22,000 lbs.

Six 14 cylinder radial BMW 801D air-cooled engines mounted in a twin-row arrangement were used to power the aircraft. Due to high altitude, the crew areas were all to be pressurized.

It could carry the Fritz X and/or the Henschel Hs 293 radio-guided bombs or missiles.

Before any useful prototypes were produced the Air Ministry dropped the project in October 1943.

Once again the victory of the Japanese at the Battle of Midway may have continued the war beyond 1945 and the Amerika Bomber may have made it to the United States.

After the war, the captured designs gave the United State a head start on our development of the X-15 rocket plane and the X-20 spaceplane. [22]

There is little doubt that if the war had continued, the V-2 weapon would have continued to bring broad destruction to England and the A9/10 may have reached the point of development that would pose a deep threat against the United States.

Documents since the war proved that with General Dornberger's leadership, Doctor Wernher von Braun was the brains behind the work of the German rockets.

By late in 1944 most scientists working on the German rocket programs, including von Braun and General Dornberger knew that Germany had lost the war and that the Russians were moving toward Peenemunde. They had to make plans to surrender to the American forces before the Russians captured them. Von Braun and several members of the engineering team, including General Dornberger, made it to Austria.

On May 2, 1945, upon finding an American private on a bicycle from the U.S. 44th Infantry Division, they surrendered. On May 3, 1945, two days before the Russians overran Peenemünde, von Braun was posing for pictures with the 44th U.S. Infantry Division.[23]

The United States Joint Chiefs of Staff established a secret recruitment program called Operation Overcast on 20 July 1945. Its purpose was to get additional military research to aid in shorting the war against the Japanese. The name Overcast was given to the German scientist's families held in Bavaria in late summer 1945. The United States Joint Intelligence Objectives Agency started a secret program called Operation Paperclip carried out by the U.S. Army Counter Intelligence Corps, moved over 1600 German scientists, engineers, and technicians to the United States.[24]

In total 88 German scientists who had worked in the design and production of rocket technology were brought to the United States. The U.S. was desperate to acquire the scientific knowledge that produced the V-1 and V-2 rockets. They had to get them before the Russians.

As the knowledge and importance of rockets became more as the war progress, if the Germans had spent more time and money on their many rockets designs, the course of the war may have changed.

Chapter 14
But What If the Japanese Had
Won at Midway?

History has proven that many events turn on things that if changed could affect the outcome of a battle and even war. A good example is the defeat of the Persians in the Battle of Marathon in 490 BC which allow the Greeks to give us their policy of democracy.

The following events led to the U.S. victory at Midway but if they had changed or not occurred the battle might have easily been won by the Japanese and could have affected the American efforts in World War II.

Six major things and events occurred that affect the Battle of Midway- 1- Japanese code-breaking, 2-use of radar by the Americans and not the Japanese, 3-the carrier Yorktown availability, 4- PBY aircraft spotting Japanese fleet, 5- Torpedo Squadron Eight flying right course and 6- Japanese destroyer leading dive bombers from carrier Enterprise to the Japanese carriers.

1. Japanese Code Breaking

Most historians would agree that the breaking of the Japanese Naval Code D, known by Americans as JN-25 was the key to victory for U.S. forces at Midway and played other parts in the war in the Pacific.

All militaries use codes during wartime to keep their communications from being read by their enemies, including the Americans. The British were busy trying to break the German codes and the Americans operating from their stations in Hawaii, named HYPO and CAST in the Philippines until it fell to the Japanese in 1942 were working on the Japanese codes.

The Germans used an electro-mechanical rotor cipher called the Enigma machine. To be able to break and read the German code you had to have the

Enigma machine, which the British did obtain. On 9 May 1941, the British Navy captured the German U boat U-110 with an Enigma machine, ciphers, and codebook. This help the British read the German codes until February 1942 when the Germans added a four-rotor into their machines.[1]

From February till October many Allied ships were lost due to the British not having the correct Enigma machine but on 30 October 1942, the British Navy captured the German U-boat U-559 with her four-rotor Enigma machine with codebooks. This event gave the British a great advantage over the Germans.[2]

The Japanese had used naval codes since the 1920s but their codes were different from the Germans, they used book ciphers. The sender and the receiver of the code both had the same codebook. The sender words and phrases are replaced with a group of letters and numbers. Additional text is encoded character by character and transmitted. The receiver looks up each group in the codebook matching the senders' and reassembles the message.

The Japanese Navy did change their codebooks regularly and in 1939 adopted the Navy General Operational Code called JN25. It was a codebook that contained 90,000 words and phrases. It was a five-digit code with a codebook to translate words into five digits. The sender used a second additive book to add additional numbers to the code. By April 1942, the Americans were able to read about 20 percent of the code which meant they could read about one in five words.

The U.S. Navy's Combat Intelligence Unit known as HYPO operated out of the basement in the old Administration Building at Pearl Harbor under the command of Lieutenant Commander Joseph Rochefort with a team of cryptanalysts and linguists.

Although the US had been successful in breaking early diplomatic Japanese codes, they were not able to break any part of the JN25 Japanese naval code till January 1942 after the surprise attack at Oahu on 7 December 1941. It is doubtable if they did break the JN25 before that date if it would have given any warning of the 7 December attack as the Japanese maintained all communication silence during the planning and operation of the attack.

By April 1942 this unit; by using IBM punch-card computers, was able to intercept, decrypt and translate parts of the Japanese radio messages within hours of when they were sent.[3]

Commander Rochefort's unit breaking Japanese messages finally determined that the Japanese referred to a future attack at 'AF' as a reference to Midway. Rochefort knowing that his job was to collect information on the enemy and pass that information to his superiors in Washington. He also knew that Washington might question his data or delay passing it to Admiral Nimitz in Hawaii. He was right as Washington did question his information and suspected the Japanese might be targeting another attack in the South Pacific instead of Midway.

Commander Rochefort had a close friend; whom he had spent three years earlier together in Japan studying the language and culture, Lieutenant Commander Edwin Layton who just happen to be Nimitz's intelligence officer. Commander Rochefort passed this information to Layton as well as Washington. Rushing this information to Admiral Nimitz allowed the Admiral to take advantage of knowing where and when the enemy would attack. This allowed Nimitz to get his forces into a position to make a surprise attack on the enemy.[4]

Before the battle, Japan had proved virtually unstoppable in the Pacific. Up until the battle at Midway, all conflicts had been initiated by the Japanese. The Japanese were making the decisions on where and when battles would be fought. After Midway, the Japanese did not initiate any new offensives, but the United States did.[5]

If the Americans had not broken the Japanese code; which Admiral Yamamoto didn't know that they had, the Japanese may have won the Battle at Midway.

2. Radar - Radio Detection and Ranging

In the 1800s, Michael Faraday; an English physicist and chemist, championed the idea that electricity and magnetic were connected. This would lead to the first electric motor. A Scottish physicist James Clerk Maxwell working on the ideas that Faraday had presented formulated the general equations of the electromagnetic field. Following up on this, German physicist Heinrich Hertz experienced with electromagnetic radiation proved that radio waves were reflected by metallic objects.

The development of this type of system that was able to produce short pulses of radio energy was the key advance that allowed modern radar systems to come into existence. During the period 1934–1939, eight nations developed in secrecy their independent radar systems, these included the United Kingdom, the United States, Germany, Japan, Russia, France, Italy, and the Netherlands.

The United States Signal Corps working with the U.S. Navy started the term Radar for these systems in 1939.

The U.S. Naval Aircraft Radio Laboratory in 1922 while conducting communication experiments along the Potomac River noticed that a wooden ship on the river was interfering with their signals. Following up on this the U.S. Naval Research Laboratory in Washington, D.C. was able to detect aircraft.[6]

The Japanese Navy did take an interest in this type of technology in the mid-1930s. They were slow in approving funding for such work. It was a feeling in the Imperial Japanese Navy that its use was highly vulnerable to enemy detection.

The Naval Research Laboratory began developing pulse radar in 1934 and started testing in 1935. The Battleship USS New York, BB-34 had the first radar installed on it in 1938. In 1940 the USS Yorktown CV-5 was the first aircraft carrier to have radar installed. Followed by the carriers Lexington CV-2, the Saratoga CV-3, the Ranger CV-4, the Enterprise CV-6, and the Wasp CV-7 in 1940.[7]

The United States Navy had radar installed on most of their ship at the Battle of Midway, including the carriers Enterprise, Hornet, and the Yorktown. This offered an early warning of approaching Japanese aircraft as the Japanese didn't have radar installed on any of their ships including their four aircraft carriers put the Japanese at a disadvantage.

It had been suggested that next to the breaking of the Japanese codes, radar was the big winner at Midway.[8]

3. Aircraft Carriers

The Battle of the Coral Sea was fought for four days in May 1942 off the northeast coast of Australia as the Japanese tried to invade Port Moresby in southeast New Guinea. It was the first air-sea battle in history with aircraft operating from aircraft carriers of both the American and Japanese navies. It was also the first sea battle where opposing force ships never saw each other.

The United States had two aircraft carriers in the South Pacific at that time, the USS Lexington and the USS Yorktown. Admiral Nimitz located in Hawaii knew the Japanese plans for the attack at Port Moresby ordered the carriers USS Enterprise and USS Hornet, which had just returned to Pearl Harbor following their raid on Tokyo with the Doolittle Raiders, to the Coral Sea. Before they could join the fight, the battle was over.

In the Japanese carrier strike force was the carrier Zuikaku and the Shokaku; the most modern fleet carriers of the Japanese navy. They were larger allowing more aircraft and heavier with more armor.

On May 7, Japanese carrier-based aircraft sunk a U.S. destroyer and an oiler. The American carrier aircraft attack and sink the Japanese light carrier Shoho and a cruiser. The next day the Japanese sunk the carrier Lexington and heavily damaged the carrier Yorktown. U.S. naval aircraft on the same day crippled the Japanese carrier Shokaku as three bombs hit the ship taken it out of action. Over half of the Japanese aircraft were lost from the carrier Zuikaku that she could no longer protect Japanese troops attempting to land at Port Moresby. The Japanese; without adequate air cover, canceled their plans for the landing at Port Moresby.

Japanese Admiral Yamamoto thinking that the carrier Yorktown had sunk, leaving the Americans with just two carriers in the Pacific, the Enterprise and Hornet. He didn't know that the Yorktown arrived back at Pearl Harbor on 27 May. Admiral Nimitz was prepared to have it repaired in record time, which he did and it sailed on 30 May for Midway.

If the U.S. carrier Yorktown had sunk at the battle of Coral Sea or had not been repaired in time for the battle of Midway, the Japanese may have won the battle of Midway.

4. PBY Out of Midway

On June 3rd at 0900 a report came in from a Navy PBY flying out of Midway, at about 500 miles west of Midway that two Japanese cargo vessels had fired on them. Officers back on Midway correctly identified these as minesweepers ahead of the Japanese main force. At 0905 another report came in from another PBY out of Midway that read "Sighted Main Body." This aircraft was about 700 miles west of Midway.

Admiral Nimitz in Hawaii; conferencing with his staff, determined this was not the main body but the invasion force. The Japanese thinking was once this force was detected, the U.S. would launch from their carriers to attack it and the Japanese would use their carrier force to attack and sink the U.S.

carriers. Nimitz didn't fall for it and held his carriers till the Japanese carriers were found.[9]

5. LCDR Waldron Torpedo Squadron

The group commander of Air Group Eight on the Hornet was Commander Stanhope Ring. His group consisted of 27 Wildcat fighters, 14 Devastator torpedo bombers, and 24 Dauntless dive bombers. Launched was scheduled for 0700, 4 June. At the morning briefing, a heading of 265 degrees at 155 miles was selected to intercept the Japanese carriers. How and why that heading was selected has not been revealed.

The torpedo planes of VT-8 under the command of Lieutenant Commander John Waldron launched last and climb to an altitude of 20,000 feet. All of the air group aircraft were in the air by 0755 and flying under radio silence. Fifteen minutes into the flight, Lcdr Waldron broke radio silence when he broadcast. "You're going in the wrong direction for the Japanese carrier force." After a brief but vocal exchange, Lcdr. Waldron said replying to another transmission from the Air Group Commander, Ring. "Well, the hell with you. I know where they are and I'm going to them." He banked his aircraft to the left and headed off in a southwest direction, followed by his entire squadron.

Lcdr. John Waldron's heading was correct and his flight flew into the Japanese carrier force.[10]

If the complete Air Group 8 including Lcdr Waldron squadron had followed the route of 265 degrees as briefed by Commander Ring, they would have missed the Japanese carrier force. This mistake could have caused the Japanese to win the Battle of Midway.

6. Japanese Destroyer Arashi

Lieutenant Commander Clarence McClusky was air group commander on the carrier USS Enterprise. He was leading 33 Dauntless dive bombers southwestward to where they thought the Japanese carrier force would be. Of the 33 dive bombers, McClusky was flying with 17 planes of Scouting Six, and 15 planes of Bombing Six. After takeoff, one of his dive bombers developed mechanical problems and returned to the ship. He continued with his flight of 32 dive bombers in what was great weather and good visibility.

At 0920 they approached the spot where they expect the Japanese carrier force to be. They found nothing but an open ocean below, not one ship was sighted. As they continued their search, fuel became a problem. Many pilots in his flight knew now that this was going to be a one-way mission due to fuel. In spike of the fuel situation, Lcdr. McClusky began a square search, turning slightly to the starboard he continued for 35 minutes flying due west, then turning right to a northwest heading, scanning the ocean and horizon for any sign of the enemy. After flying northwest for 15 minutes he turned right to a northeast heading. All of his group aircraft were still with him except two who had to ditch because of fuel.

After flying at 20,000 feet for an extended time, some pilots and crew began to run low on oxygen, McClusky ordered a descent to 15,000 feet so they didn't need oxygen.

Well north of where they expected to have incepted the enemy fleet at 0955, McClusky noticed a ship making big waves, heading north at a high rate of speed. Suspecting this was a Japanese ship hurrying north to catch up with the main Japanese carrier force, McClusky turned his flight to follow the wake of the ship, and he headed north. At 10:05 small dark specks appeared on the ocean surface, he had found the long source after Japanese carrier force that he had almost missed.[11]

If Lcdr McClusky's flight of 32 dive bombers had turned back when their fuel was low, they would have missed the Japanese Destroyer Arashi making waves toward the main Japanese carrier force. His dive bombers would not have attack and sunk the Japanese carriers, Akagi and Kaga. The results of this battle may have been in the Japanese flavor.

As discussed in the chapter on the Atlantic Fleet, if the Japanese won the battle of Midway and they controlled the central and eastern Pacific Ocean, President Roosevelt would have no choice but to send both naval vessels and military troops from the mainland of the United States to protect the Hawaii Islands and the west coast of the United States. He had enough troops to spare but the availability of naval ships was another question. If the United States was to continue to support the convoys from the U.S. and Canada to Great Britain, the president would have to keep some of the Atlantic Fleet destroyers in the Atlantic for the convoy patrols and to use to protect larger ships moving through the Panama Canal and the Strait of Magellan at Cape Horn in South America.

If President Roosevelt was forced to move ships, crews, and soldiers from the States to protect the Pacific and the war continued beyond 1945, the German secret weapons may have played a role in the outcome of World War II.

Epilogue

Many historians studying the Battle of Midway; as pointed out in the prologue, thought that the Japanese should have won that battle. A victory by the Japanese may have delayed the war beyond 1945. A review of the many weapons Germany had in their pipeline could have changed the course of the war.

German scientists were working on many different weapons before, during, and after the war. Some were strange but some; if time had allowed, may have produced better results for the Germans. Many after the war became valuable to the United States space program.

This book has tried to point out the German weapons that could have played a role in the results of World War II if the Japanese had been victorious at the Battle of Midway.

Notes

Introduction

[1] Naval War College Review-Review Essay by Thomas Wildenberg

[2] Naval War College Review-Review Essay

[3] Incredible Victory by Walter Lord 1967

[4] Walter Johnson, The Battle Against Isolation, (Chicago University of Chicago Press, 1944), pp. 247

[5] Harold Callender, "Two Oceans, Two Worlds," New York Times, 6 Oct 1940

[6] Hearings Before the Joint Committee on the Investigations of the Pearl Harbor Attack, 79th Congress, 1st session, p

[7] The Nauticapedia-An Overview of Royal Canadian Navy Fishermen's Reserve-by John M. MacFarlane 2012

[8] See Morison, History of United States Naval

Chapter 1 - Fear of Invasion

[1] Japan's Decision for War, p 153 in quotes from Ike.

[2] From Mahan to Pearl Harbor, p 267 as quoted in Asada

[3] War History Office, National Defense College, Senshi sousho hawai sakusen (Military history series: Hawaii strategy)

[4] Stephan, Hawaii under the Rising Sun & Parshall and Tully, Shattered Sword.

[5] Fuchida and Okumiya, Midway, chs. I-VII.

[6] AAF Monograph 41, Operational History of the Seventh Air Force, p. 105.

[7] Leighton and Coakley, Global Logistics and Strategy, 1940-43, PP. 146-49

[8] Rad, CofS to CG Hawaiian Dept, 1 Apr 42, OPD 452.1Hawaii/26; OPD Weekly Status Map, Mar-June 42, OPD Exec file

[9] Allen, Hawaii's War Years, pp. 151-54; Memo, ASGS for CofS, 19 Feb 42, in OCS Conf, binder 33

[10] Memo, ACofS WPD for CofS, 12 Dec 41, WPD 4622-37

[11] General Headquarters Supreme Commander for the Allied Powers, Japan, Japanese Operations in the Southwest Pacific Area (Southwest Pacific Series, vol. II), National Archives and Records Service, p. 70

[12] List of Sub-Carried Plane Strikes, prepared by the Japanese Navy, in Pearl Harbor Attack pt. 13, pp. 650-51.

[13] Allen, Hawaii's War Years, p. 59

[14] John A. Rademaker, These Are Americans: The Japanese Americans in Hawaii in World War II (Palo Alto, Calif.: Pacific Books, 1951

[15] TAG to CG Hawaiian Dept, 2 Feb 42, Rad, CG Hawaiian Dept to TAG, 4 Feb 42. Both in WPD 4250-5.

[16] Lind, Hawaii's Japanese, PP-78-79, 108-09.

[17] Notes on Conf at White House (President and American advisers only), 28 Dec 41, WDCSA 334 Mtgs and Confs (1-28-42).

[18] Temporarily, with the establishment of the unity of command on 17 Dec 1941.

[19] Notes, War Council Mtg, 23 Mar 42, in SW Conf, Binder Two.

[20] Stimson Diary, entry of 21 Apr 42. p. 88

[21] War Council Mtg, 23 Mar 42, in SW Conf, Binder 2;

[22] Memo, ASW McCloy for SW, 1 Apr 42, WDCSA 42-43 Haw.

Chapter 2 - Midway

[1] pubs.usgs.gov-gig-dynamic-Hawaiian

[2] Friend of Midway Atoll-Honoring the Past.

[3] Gandt, Robert L. (1995) Skygods: The Fall of Pan Am

[4] Encyclopedia Britannica -Article-"Battle of Midway" written by Michael Ray

[5] Morison, Vol. III, 59; Fuchida, 66-71, 76; Willmott, 8-9, 16, 33. Willmott records passage of the Naval Expansion Act in June 1940

[6] Naval War College-Japanese Operational Plans in World War II - Shortfalls in Critical Elements by Lcdr Tomas Culora.

[7] Fuchida, The Battle of Midway that Doomed Japan, p78

[8] Nimitz Command Summary, 16 May 1942, HCIVWII.2.2

[9] Lurren msg 440Z May 1942, CINCPAC message file,RG38, NA

[10] Fuchida, 86; Willmott, 343; and Morison, Samuel: History of US Naval Operations of WWII, Vol. IV, 84

[11] Naval History and Heritage Command-Japanese Story of the Battle of Midway OPNAVP32-1002

[12] Shattered Sword, The Untold Story of the Battle of Midway by J. Parshall & A. Tully, 2005, p55-56

[13] The Battle of Midway, World War 2 Facts

[14] Muir, Malcolm (October 1990). "Rearming in a Vacuum: United States Navy Intelligence and The Japanese Capital Ship Threat, 1936-1945

[15] Baker, Benjamin David (2016) "What if Japan Had Won".

Chapter 3 - Japan

[1] Arisawa, Hiromi, ed, Nihon Keizaishi 1 (History Japanese Industries, vol. 1) 1994

[2] Owlcation-Humanities-History of Japan-May 19, 2020

[3] rekishinihon.com/2013/05/10/edict of 1635-Japanese History and Culture

[4] The Dawn of History to the Late Tokugawa Period, edited by David J. Lu Armonk

[5] Van Zandt, Howard (1984, Pioneer American Merchants in Japan, p 13

[6] English Wikipedia on Preble Logbook

[7] Naval History and Heritage Command—Commodore Matthews C. Perry and the Opening of Japan

[8] Matthews C. Perry by Editors of Encyclopedia Britannic

[9] Encyclopedia Britannica—Meiji Restoration—Japanese History

[10] The Taft-Katsura Agreement-Reality or Myth by Ramond A. Esthus, p 46-51

[11] Japanese Militarism-Wikipedia

[12] This Day in History by History Channel-21 February 1944

[13] American Historical Association—"Why Did Japan Chose War"

[14] Japan: A Documentary History by David John Lu, August 1997, p 439

[15] Shinmin no Michi from Wikipedia

[16] Pearl Harper Mini-Q "Why Did Japan Attack Pearl Harbor"

[17] History.com-This day in history-12 December 1937, USS Panay is sunk by the Japanese

[18] World War 2 headquarters.com-Greater East Asia Co-Prosperity Sphere

[19] Asia for Educators, Columbia University-Japan's Quest for Power in WWII in Asia.

[20] Diplomatic Background of the Pearl Harbor Attack-Part I, Foreign Relations, vol. II, p 343

[21] New York Times-A Reluctant Enemy-Opinion Piece 12/2011

[22] Your Dictionary-Isoroku Yamamoto Facts

[23] HistoryNet-Article "Gentlemanly Warfare is Dead."

[24] Naval History and Heritage Command-Ch 5-The Battle of Midway.

[25] Naval History and Heritage Command-Battle of Midway Interrogations of Japanese Officials

[26] Oregon. gov-archives-Bombs Fall on Oregon: Japanese Attack on State.

Chapter 4 - China

[1] *Wikipedia.org/w/index.php?title-Demography of the Japan&oldid=957940042*

[2] Michael M. Walker, The 1929 Sinco-Soviet War: The War Nobody Knew, p 1

[3] Encyclopedia Britannica, "Chinese Eastern Railway, railway, China." Retrieved 11 December 2016

[4] Editors of Encyclopedia Britannica article Nationalist Party

Chapter 5 - United States

[1] Thought.Com "The Evolution of American Isolationism"

[2] Sect of State, Office of the Historian Ari American Isolationism in the 1930s

[3] Joint Military Intelligence College-"Courting a Reluctant Allied" by Lcdr Gregory Florence, USN

[4] *AFE.easia.colimbia.edu/special/japan*

[5] United States-British Staff Conversations Report, (ABC-1), on the Investigations of the Pearl Harbor Attack, 79th Congress, 1st session, (Washington, 1946), pp. 1492.

[6] Thomas F. Troy, *Wild Bill, and Intrepid: Donovan, Stephenson, and the Origin of the CIA* (New Haven, Conn.: Yale University Press, 1996), 19-30, 48-56

[7] N. R. Hitchcock, CDR, USN, Assistant Naval Attaché for Air on Captain Kirk papers.

[8] Bath, 27-28; MacLachlan, 225-226; Smith, Ultra-Magic Deals, 14-16; Dorwart, Conflict of Duty, 144

[9] Fireside Chat on National Security, 29 December 1940, Public Papers and Addresses of Franklin D. Roosevelt

[10] Steven Casey, Cautious Crusade: Franklin D. Roosevelt, American Public Opinion, and the War Against Nazi Germany, pp. 215

[11] *History,army.mil/book-sub*: Joint Basic War Plan

[12] Warfare History Network-Expanding the size of the Military in WWII

Chapter 6 - Great Britain

[1] Anglotopia for Anglophiles-Brit History: The Rise of the British Empire in the Tudor and Elizabethan Age by John Rabon

[2] Geoffrey Parker, "The 'Dreadnought' Revolution of Tudor England", Vol. 82 Issue 3, pp 269-300

[3] Fox, Gregory H. (2008). Humanitarian Occupation,p23-29,35,60

[4] Johnson, Douglas: Reisman, Michael: The Historical Foundation of World Order, p508-510

[5] *Cambridge.org/core/books/Kaiser/dreams-of-a-german-europe* by Roderick McLean

[6] *History.com*: This day in History, April 6, 1971

[7] Yutaka, Kawasaki (7 August 1996) "Was 1910 Annexation Treaty Between Korea and Japan Concluded Legally?"

[8] *Hisory.com*: This day in History, March 7, 1936

[9] History Channel - This day in History, Germany annexes Austria.

[10] BBC History Magazine: The Munich Agreement-The Battle over Appeasement

[11] History Channel: Battle of Dunkirk-Jan 25, 2018

[12] Arthur J. Marder, From the Dardanelles to Iran (Annapolis, MD: Naval Institute Press, 2015), p. 106.

[13] BBC-The German Threat to Britain in World War II by Dan Cruickshank, 2011-06021

[14] International Churchill Society-Churchill speech 1940-Their Finest Hour

[15] *der-fuehrer.org/redden/English/wardirectives*

[16] Ibid

[17] Battle of Britain, European History by The Editors of Encyclopedia Britannica

[18] Churchill Society of London-"The Few' Churchill's speeches to the House of Commons 8/20/1940

[19] "Days of Infamy" by John Costello (1994) published by Simon and Schuster

[20] *Pacificwar.org.au/Germany* First article by James Bowen

[21] Winston S. Churchill 1948, The Grand Alliance, Rosetta Books p.23.

[22] Harold Callender, "Two Oceans, Two Worlds," New York Times, 6 Oct 1940.

[23] Ibid

[24] U.S. Congress, Hearings Before the Joint Committee on the Investigations of the Pearl Harbor Attack, 79th Congress, 1st session, (Washington, 1946), pp. 1492.

Chapter 7 - The Atlantic Fleet

[1] Wikipedia-United States Fleet Forces Command

[2] NasSource Naval History-Locations of Warships of the United States Navy December 7, 1941

[3] *usmm.org/shipsunk*: damaged-Merchant Ships sunk in WWII

[4] *history.com-Lend-Lease Act* dated 4 Nov 2019

[5] BBC History Magazine-The Battle of the Atlantic: why Britain almost lost to Hitler's U-boats

[6] Warfare History-Undeclared War in the Atlantic by James I. Marino

[7] Morrison, Samuel Elliot, *History of United States Naval Operations in World War II, Volume One: The Battle of the Atlantic, September 1939-May 1943*

[8] Naval History and the Heritage Command-United States Atlantic Fleet Organization-1942

Chapter 8 - Germany

[1] Museum of WWII, From War to War in Europe 1919-1939

[2] Yadvashem.org article

[3] Mein Kampf, work by Hitler-The Editors of Encyclopedia Britannica

[4] *history.com/this-day-in-history/germany-launches-operation-barbarossathe-invasion-of-russia*

[5] *history.com/news/d-day-roosevelt-churchill-doubts-planning*

[6] *encyclopedia.ushmm.ogr* - Operation Torch: The Anglo-American Invasion of French North Africa

Chapter 9 - German Weapons

[1] The Nobel Prize - Nobel Prize in Physics 1932.

[2] *https://www.wikiwand.com/en/Wunderwaffe*

[3] Killen, John (2003), The Luftwaffe: A History, Barnsley, South Yorkshire: Pen & Sword Books, p 93

[4] Tammen 1978, p 195

[5] Boyne 1994, p 325

[6] Smithsonian-National Air & Space-Bomb, Guided, Fritz X (X-1)

[7] Smith and Kay 1972, p 234 Donald 1999, p.494.

[8] Mark Peattie, Sunburst: The Rise of Japanese Naval Air Power, 1909-1941, p 94

[9] Nowarra, Heinz J (1980), Heinkel He 111: A documentary History

[10] Mackay, Ron (2003), Heinkel He 111, Crowood Aviation series

[11] Griehl, Manfred; Dressel, Joachim (1998). Heinkel He 177-277-274. Shrewsbury, England: Airlife Publishing. p. 232.

[12] Dressel and Griehl 1994, p.95

[13] Vernaleken, M. Handig (2006). Junkers Ju 388: Development, Testing, and Production of the Last Junkers High-Altitude Aircraft

[14] Angelucci, Enzo. The Rand McNally Encyclopedia Of Military Aircraft, 1914-1980 (1988) 546pp

[15] Taylor, Michael J H. Jane's Encyclopedia of Aviation. pg. 825

[16] Smithsonian: National Air and Space: Arado Ar 196

[17] Green, William. Warplanes of the Third Reich. London: Macdonald and Jane's Publishers Ltd., 4th impression n1979, p.56, 78-80

[18] Ibid

[19] Ford, Roger (2013) Germany's Secret Weapons of World War II, p 224

[20] Smith, J. Richard. Dornier Do 335: The Luftwaffe's Fastest Piston-Engine Fighter (Classic Publications, 2007).

[21] Nowarra 1993, p. 189.

[22] Wagner, Ray: Nowarra, Heinz (1971) German Combat Planes: A Comprehensive Survey and History of the Development of German Military Aircraft from 1914 to 1945, p 229

[23] Donald 1994, p. 221

[24] West, Jim. "*Me 410A-2/U1 FE-499 www.indianamilitary.org*.

[25] Hyland p 219, 221

[26] Green, William (2010). Aircraft of the Third Reich. Vol.1

[27] "The Focke-Wulf Ta 152" *archive.org* Retrieved8 February 2011

[28] Green & Swanborough 1988, p 25

[29] Angelucci, Enzo (1988). Combat aircraft of World War II. P. 50

[30] Christopher, John. The Race for Hitler's X-Planes p 145

[31] Heinkel He 219#cite note-Boyne 1997, p295

[32] *http://www.historyofwar.org/articles/weapons: henschel hs 129.html*

[33] *http://www.luft46.com/prototype/berlin9.html*

[34] Christopher, John. The Race for Hitler's X-Planes (The Mill, Gloucestershire: History Press, 2013), p 147.

[35] Green, William (1970). The warplanes of the Third Reich

[36] *https://www.nationalmuseum.af.mil/Visit/Museum-Exhibits/Fact-sheets/Display/Article/196266/messerschmitt-me-262a-schwalbe/*

[37] *https://airandspace.si.edu/collection-objects/arado-ar-234-b-2-blitz-lightning/nasm*

[38] *https://military.wikia.org/wiki/Messerschmitt_Me_264*

[39] Military Factory-Messerschmitt Me 163 Komet 2/10/2020

[40] Toliver, Raymond F.; Constable, Trevor J.(1996). Fighter Aces of the Luftwaffe.

[41] "Zeppelin "Rammer" Luft '46 entry

Chapter 10 – Secret Weapons of Nazi Germany

[1] *https://www.britannica.com/topic/IG-Farben*

[2] Chemical & Engineering News-The Nazi Origin of deadly Nerve Gases-by Sarah Everts Oct 17, 2016.

[3] *https://www.britannica.com/topic/United-Steelworks-Co*

[4] *Britannica.com/topic/Krupp-AG*

[5] *Britannica.com/biography/Hugo-Junkers*

[6] Griehl, Manfred, Dressel, Joachim, Heineken He 177, p 54

[7] *Wikipedia.org/wiki/Messerschmitt*

[8] *Google.com/Scientists/Germany/WorldWar II*

[9] Warfare History Network-Hitler, World War II, Technology, Jets, 7 December 2019

[10] *uboataces.com* - German U-Boat: Rocket U-Boat Program

[11] *uboat.net* - U-Boat types

[12] *SeacoastNH.com* article Nazi U-boats Surrender at Portsmouth

[13] *Militaryhistorynow.com*-Fantastic Flattops-Three Amazing Aircraft Carriers that Might Have Changed History.

[14] *Tanks-encyclopedia.com* - German Tanks of WW2

[15] Spielberger, Walter J., and Uwe Feist. Sturmartillerie. Fallbrook, CA. Aero, 1967.

[16] German Tanks of World War II, The complete Illustrated History of German Armored Fighting Vehicles 1926-1945, F,M von Senger and Etterlin

[17] Parada, George: "Panzer VIII Maus" Achtung Panzer

[18] FitzGerald, Michael (10 September 2018). Hitler's Secret Weapons of Mass Destruction: The Nazis' Plan for Final Victory

[19] White, B.T. (1983). Tanks and other Armored Fighting Vehicles of World War II, New York: Exeter Books, pp 298-299.

[20] *https://www.militaryfactory.com/armor/details.asp?armor*

[21] *https://tanks-encyclopedia.com/ww2/nazi_germany SD-Kfz-164_Nashorn.php*

[22] Haupt, W. (1990) (1989). Panzerabwehrgeschütze 1935-1945 (German Anti-Tank Guns *1935-1945*).

[23] YouTube video by Mark Felton Productions-https://www.youtube.com/watch?v=MRDnJ-Kbk8

[24] *NationalInterest.com* - Nazi Germany's V-3 Super Gun, The Ultimate Terror Weapon. By Sebastien Roblin 1/8/2017

[25] American Arsenal: A Century of Weapon Technology by Patrick Coffey, Oxford University Press 2014, p 152-54

[26] *https://interestingengineering.com/schwerer-gustav-the-biggest-cannon-during-wwii*

[27] American Arsenal: A Century of Weapon Technology by Patrick Coffey, Oxford University Press 2014, p 152-54

[28] Hechler, Ken: The Bridge at Remagen; A Story of World War II (First ed) Presidio Press

[29] *https://cen.acs.org/articles/94/i41/Nazi-origins-deadly-nerve-gases.html*

[30] *https://www.history.com/news/the-nazis-developed-sarin-Gas*

[31] Stanley P. Lovell, Of Spies & Stratagems(Englewood Cliffs, New Jersey: Prentice-Hall, 1963), p. 78.21-220

[32] Arthur H. Compton to James B. Conant (15 July 1942), Bush-Conant file, Roll 7, Target 10, Folder 75, "Espionage."

[33] Manhattan District History, Book 1, Volume 14, Foreign Intelligence Supplement No. 2 (Peppermint), 31 July 1952

[34] *Wikipedia, the free encyclopedia-The Bergius process*

[35] Coal Gasification & Co-production of Chemicals & Fuels by Daniel Cicero 2007-06-11

Chapter 11 – Other Weapons

[1] Estes, Kenneth W (2014). Super-heavy Tanks of World War II. Oxford, UK: Osprey Publishing.

[2] Whitley, M. J. (1998). Battleships of World War II. Annapolis: Naval Institute Press, p. 90.

[3] Garzke, William H. & Dulin, Robert O. 1985). Battleships: Axis and Neutral Battleships in World War II. Annapolis: Naval Institute Press

[4] Whitey, p.90.2

[5] Garzke & Dulin, p. 312

[6] Aircraft of the Luftwaffe 1935-1945, Jean-Denis G.G.

[7] Dressel and Griehl 1994, p. 25

[8] *https://www.warhistoryonline.com/instant- articles/messerschmitt-323.html*

[9] forgettweapons.com/wp-content/uploads/2013/10/SdKfz251Falke-night-vision

[10] Gotz, Hans Dieter, German Military Rifles and Machine Pistols, 1871-1945, (1990) p 170

[11] *https://world-war-2.wikia.org/wiki/Fliegerfaust*

[12] *flyingheritage.org/Explore/The-Collection/Germany/ Fieseler-Fi-103R*

[13] "Moments in Helicopter History" by Hermann Ganswindt-Archived from the original on 10 August 2016.

[14] *Britannica.com/technology/helicopter* - written by Walter James Boyne

[15] *defensemedianetwork.com/stories/nazi-rotors-german-helicopter-development-1932-1945-flettner.*

[16] *Warhistoryonline.com/war-articles/german-secret-weapons-of-wwii.* By Jack Beckett 6 April 2014

[17] *warhistoryonline.com/war-articles/german-secret-weapons-of-wwii.*

By Jack Beckett 6 April 2014

[18] Lexikon der Wehrmacht Sturmgewehre-Encyclopedia of the German Army: Assault Rifles-Wehrmacht 1/11/2007

[19] *warhistoryonline.com/war-articles/german-secret-weapons-of-wwii.* By Apr 6, 2014 Jack Beckett

[20] 'Die Glocke' by Rob Arndt (1945) http://bell.greyfalcon.us/Glocke.htm/

[21] "Intercept But Don't Shoot" by Dr. Renato Vesco, Grove Press 1971

[22] *https://www.iwm.org.uk/history/the-incredible-story-of-the-dambusters-raid*

[23] Mechanix Illustrated, April 1944-Nazi Secret Weapons of WWII

[24] The Online Tank Museum-Kugelpanzer 25 September, 2016-Article by Mark Nash

Chapter 12 - Atomic Bomb & Rocket Program

[1] See Morison, History of United States Naval Operations in World War II, Volume I, pp. 47. 7

[2] American Heritage Foundation Einstein-Szilard Letter.

[3] Atomic Heritage Foundation-German Atomic Bomb Project 10/18/2016

[4] The Making of the Atomic Bomb by Richard Rhodes 1986

[5] Werner Heisenberg-Facts. NobelPrize.org. Nobel Media AB 2020.

[6] Article from WWII Museum—War to War in Europe 1919-1939

[7] U.S. National Archives, Interrogation of Albert Speer, 11 June 1945 RG 331, Entry 18A

[8] Atomic Heritage Foundation-Morris "Moe" Berg

[9] Ref *https://en.wikipedia.org/wiki/Rainer_Karlsch*

Chapter 13 - Germany's Rocket Program

[1] Wikipedia, the free encyclopedia-Werner von Braun

[2] Britannica-Walter Robert Dornberger by Editors of Encyclopedia Britannica

[3] Britannica-the Peenemunde by the Editors of Encyclopedia Britannica

[4] Wikipedia, the free encyclopedia-Werner von Braun

[5] Inside the Third Reich" by Albert Speer.

[6] http://www.astronautix.com/s/schmetterling.html

[7] http://www.luft46.com/missile/wasserfl.html

[8] Ref Fiesler Fi103 (V1) - Royal Air Force Museum, Cosford (UK)

[9] Gander, Terry, and Chamberlain, Peter. Weapons of the Third Reich.

[10] *https://dbpedia.org/page/Aggregat-(rocket-family*

[11] Dornberger, Walter (1954). V-2. New York: The Viking Press, Inc.

[12] Ibid

[13] *https://www.nasa.gov/centers/marshall/history/vonbraun/bio.html*

[14] *http://www.astronautix.com/r/raketenflugplatz.html*

[15] Inside the Third Reich" by Albert Speer.

[16] *https://en.wikipedia.org/wiki/V-2_rocket*

[17] *https://www.subbrit.org.uk/sites/nordhausen-v2-factory-and-dora-concentration-camp/*

[18] Dornberger, Walter (1954). V-2. New York: The Viking Press, Inc.

[19] *http://www.astronautix.com/r/rheinbote.html*

[20] *http://www.astronautix.com/a/a9a10.html*

[21] Dornberger, Walter (1954). V-2. New York: The Viking Press, Inc.

[22] Sänger, Eugen (1933). Rocket Flight Engineering. (Washington, 1965): NASA Tech. Trans. F-223.

[23] *wikipedia.org/wiki/Wernher von Braun Surrender to the American*

[24] Esquire article - *Hunters'* Nazi NASA Scientists Are Based on the True Story of Operation Paperclip by Gabrielle Bruney

Chapter 14 - What if the Japanese had Won at Midway

[1] *theguardian.com/world/2017/oct/20/enigma-code*

[2] Ibid

[3] *Slate.com* - How Did the U.S. Break Japanese Military Codes before the Battle of Midway? By Andrew Warinner

[4] National Security Agency/Central Security Service-'AF' Identified as Code for Midway

[5] The Battle of Midway by Craig Symonds, Oxford University Press, 2011

[6] Raymond C. Watson, Jr.; Radar Origins Worldwide, Trafford Publishing, 2009.

[7] U.S. Institute-The Launch of Navy Radar, December 29, 2015 by Norman Friedman

[8] U.S. Naval Research Laboratory-Highlights Radar Accomplishments during Midway, by Jonathan Sunderman, June 4, 2017.

[9] The Battle of Midway by Craig Symonds, Oxford University Press, 2011.

[10] Ibid

[11] Ibid